*Mrs. Twemlow*

# POETRY

*Plus*

*Meguido Zola*

Copp Clark Pitman Ltd.
A Longman Company

ISBN 0-7730-4703-4

**Editing**  Sheila Fletcher, Linda Scott

**Design**  Rob McPhail

**Illustration**  Harvey Chan: 6-11; Rob McPhail: 14-19;
Craig Terlson: 22-27; Don Gauthier: 30-35, 70-75; Karen
Evans: 38-43; Dominique Prévost: 46-51; Susan Leopold:
54-59, 102-107; Maureen Paxton: 62-67, 110-115; Darcia
Labrosse: 78-83; David Cousins: 86-91; Susanna Denti: 94-
99; Victor Gad: 118-123

**Typesetting**  Compeer Typographic Services Limited

**Printing and binding**  John Deyell Company

We gratefully acknowledge the contribution of Lynda
Pogue in the early development stages of this project.

Copp Clark Pitman Ltd.
2775 Matheson Blvd. East
Mississauga, Ontario
L4W 4P7

Printed and bound in Canada

*For poets, mentors, and friends:*

David Booth
Angela Dereume
Marsha Ivany
Janice Leyland
Sheila Luetzen
Cheryl MacLeod
Suzie Montabello
Marion Rumble
Jean Way
and
Melanie Zola

# CONTENTS

# WHAT'S A POEM, ANYWAY???

**By Yourself**

- *Think!* Have you ever
  —heard a poem?
  —read a poem?
  —written a poem?
- Make a list of as many things that you can think of that would describe or define a poem—these could be words, phrases, or sentences.
- What do poems sound like? How do they look? Do poems rhyme? Do they have a beat? What do people tell or write about in poems? How do poems make you feel? What do you like (or not like) about poetry?

**With a Partner**

- Read your lists to each other.
- Together, choose three of four things from your lists that best describe a poem.
- Put these on cards or strips of paper.
- Get ready to tell the class about your ideas.

**With the Whole Class**

- Design a "What's a poem anyway?" bulletin board and display your thoughts and ideas.

## Chocolate

Chocolate
Chocolate
      I
love
   you so
      I
want
     to
marry
     you
     and
live
   forever
        in the
         flavor
of your
brown

*Arnold Adoff*

## Poem for Aelurophobe

S-s-scatcat

*Marah Gilead*

## Place Names

Bella Bella, Bella Coola,
Athabaska, Iroquois;
Mesilinka, Osilinka,
Mississauga, Missisquois.
Chippewa, Chippawa,
Nottawasaga;
Oshawa, Ottawa,
Nassagaweya;
Malagash, Matchedash,
Shubenacadie;
Couchiching, Nippissing,
Scubenacadie.
Shickshock
Yahk
Quaw!

*Meguido Zola*

## Gift Wrapped

What would we do without a skin
for us to keep our innards in?

*Inge Israel*

# What the 500 Kilogram Canary Said

kitty kitty kitty kitty kitty kitty kitty kitty kitty kitty kitty kitty kitty kit
tty kitty kitty kitty kitty kitty kitty kitty kitty kitty kitty kitty kitty kitty
y kitty kitty kitty kitty kitty kitty kitty kitty kitty kitty kitty kitty kitty k
kitty kitty kitty kitty kitty kitty kitty kitty kitty kitty kitty kitty kitty kit
tty kitty kitty kitty kitty kitty kitty kitty kitty kitty kitty kitty kitty kitty
y kitty kitty kitty kitty kitty kitty kitty kitty kitty kitty kitty kitty kitty k
kitty kitty kitty kitty kitty kitty kitty kitty kitty kitty kitty kitty kitty kit
tty kitty kitty kitty kitty kitty kitty kitty kitty kitty kitty kitty kitty kitty
y kitty kitty kitty kitty kitty kitty kitty kitty kitty kitty kitty kitty kitty k
kitty kitty kitty kitty kitty kitty kitty kitty kitty kitty kitty kitty kitty kit
tty kitty kitty kitty kitty kitty kitty kitty kitty kitty kitty kitty kitty kitty
y kitty kitty kitty kitty kitty kitty kitty kitty kitty kitty kitty kitty kitty k
kitty kitty kitty kitty kitty kitty kitty kitty kitty kitty kitty kitty kitty kit
tty kitty kitty kitty kitty kitty kitty kitty kitty kitty kitty kitty kitty kitty
y kitty kitty kitty kitty kitty kitty kitty kitty kitty kitty kitty kitty kitty k
kitty kitty kitty kitty kitty kitty kitty kitty kitty kitty kitty kitty kitty kit
tty kitty kitty kitty kitty kitty kitty kitty kitty kitty kitty kitty kitty kitty
y kitty kitty kitty kitty kitty kitty kitty kitty kitty kitty kitty kitty kitty k
kitty kitty kitty kitty kitty kitty kitty kitty kitty kitty kitty kitty kitty kit
tty kitty kitty kitty kitty kitty kitty kitty kitty kitty kitty kitty kitty kitty
y kitty kitty kitty kitty kitty kitty kitty kitty kitty kitty kitty kitty kitty k
kitty kitty kitty kitty kitty kitty kitty kitty kitty kitty kitty kitty kitty kit
tty kitty kitty kitty kitty kitty kitty kitty kitty kitty kitty kitty kitty kitty
y kitty kitty kitty kitty kitty kitty kitty kitty kitty kitty kitty kitty kitty k

*Marah Gilead*

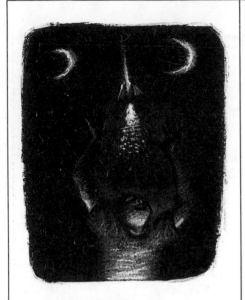

## 5–4–3

5
4
3
2
1 rocket
2 the moon
3 flew it
what 4?
5
4
3
2
1 rocket

*Michael Rosen*

## Lost

. . . . . . ? . . . . . .

*Shaunt Basmajian*

# Dad and the Cat and the Tree

This morning a cat got
Stuck in our tree.
Dad said, "Right, just
Leave it to me."

The tree was wobbly,
The tree was tall.
Mum said, "For goodness'
Sake don't fall!"

"Fall?" scoffed Dad,
"A climber like me?
Child's play, this is!
You wait and see."

He got out the ladder
From the garden shed.
It slipped. He landed
in the flower bed.

"Never mind," said Dad,
Brushing the dirt
Off his hair and his face
And his trousers and his shirt.

"Fall again?" said Dad.
"Funny joke!"
Then he swung himself up
On a branch.  It broke.

Dad landed **wallop**
Back on the deck.
Mum said, "Stop it,
You'll break your neck!"

"We'll try Plan B. Stand
Out of the way!"
Mum said, "Don't fall
Again, O.K.?"

"Rubbish!" said Dad.
"Now we'll try Plan C.
Easy as winking
To a climber like me!"

Then he climbed up high
On the garden wall.
Guess what?
He **didn't fall!**

## Canada Day

Canada Day:

after all the fireworks, the stars

still there

*George Swede*

He gave a great leap
And he landed flat
In the crook of the tree
Right on the cat!

The cat gave a yell
And sprang to the ground,
Pleased as Punch to be
Safe and sound.

So it's smiling and smirking
Smug as can be,
But poor Dad's
Still

Stuck
Up
The
Tree!

*Kit Wright*

## Nature

As the orange-
striped cat
hunches
glaring down,

the pale-fluffed
nestlings
he's discovered
feel cooled
in the shadow,

and

stretch their thin
necks, heavy
heads up,
hungry
beaks open,

wide
on hinges.

*Milton Acorn*

Well, what is a poem anyway?

The truth is that poems can be all kinds of things. They can be about almost anything and everything. And they can sound like and look like just about anything.

Anyone and everyone can write a poem. If you've ever remembered a good time, thought about a hobby, talked about something that you believed, written a thank-you letter or dreamt about a trip you were taking, then you can create a poem.

Poems say something. People create poetry to express something—a thought or a feeling. And to tell about these things. Poems are jokes, complaints, prayers, observations, recipes, hopes, plans, insults, memories, boasts, advertisements—and even love letters (like Arnold Adoff's love note and marriage proposal to chocolate).

And poems come in all sorts of shapes and patterns and forms—from nursery rhymes to haiku, and limericks to ballads.

Poetry comes in all kinds of sizes, too. The longest poem in the world has almost as many words as there are children in Canada.

1. *In a Small Group*
   - Read aloud the poems in Collection 1 again.
   - Talk about them. What did you like or not like about each? Why?

2. *a) By Yourself*
   - Choose a poem you like.
   - Say it to yourself four or five times; try out different ways of reciting it.
   - Copy it onto a sheet of paper.

| | |
|---|---|
| **b) With a Partner** | • Read or say your poem to a partner. |
| | • Ask your partner what he or she felt about the poem. |
| | • Now, listen to your partner's poem and tell how you felt about it. |
| **3. With the Whole Class** | • Take another look at the "What's a poem anyway?" bulletin board. |
| | • Can you add any more thoughts on what a poem is? Do you still agree with all of your first thoughts? |
| **4.a) By Yourself** | • Choose one of the poems in the Collection as a model for a poem of your own. How would your poem be similar? different? |
| | • Write out your poem in rough. |
| **b) With a Partner** | • Exchange poems and read each other's, silently and out loud. |
| | • Tell each other if you can see what the connections are between the poem from the Collection and the new poem. |
| | • Help each other to improve the poems. |
| **c) By Yourself** | • On a large sheet of paper, make a good copy of your own poem and your chosen poem from the Collection. Share your work with the class. |
| **5.a) By Yourself or With a Partner** | • Find some funny? sad? unusual? scary? wonderful? poems. |
| | • Copy them or tape record them for the rest of the class. |

# JEST JOKING

*By Yourself*

*Try to remember:*
What is the funniest joke you've ever heard?
- Write it down.
- Practise saying it. Use lots of expression.
- Don't forget to pause before the punch line.
- When you're ready, tell your joke to the class. (Perhaps your class could start a "Do You Need a Laugh?" audio tape.)

*By Yourself*

- Begin to collect different kinds of jokes and riddles from friends outside your classroom. Collect them from your family too.
- They may be funny or not-so-funny (or different kinds of funny!).
- Whenever you hear a *really* good joke, type it or write it out carefully. Hang it on the "Joke Tree."

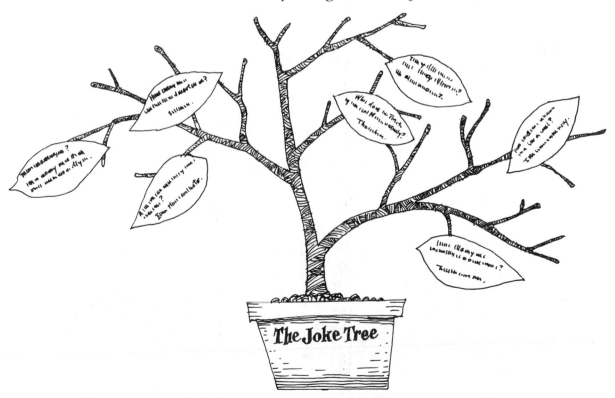

The Joke Tree

## Apple for Teacher

*Meguido Zola*

## Who Was Left?

Pete and Repete were whizzing around on the roller-coaster. Pete flew off. Who was left?
**Repete.**
Okay. Pete and Repete were whizzing around . . .

*Collected by Brandy Longstaffe, Vancouver, British Columbia.*

## Batty Books

WHERE'S MY SOCK? BY SONYA FOOTE

DON'T WAKE BABY! BY ELSIE CRYZE

OFF TO THE CIRCUS By I. Felix Cited

THE SURGEON BY E. DREW BLOOD

VACATION BY HOLLY DAY

Rice Growing By Paddy Fields

GONE WITH THE WIND By Gale Force

*Collected by Ralph Smith, Fort McMurray, Alberta*

# What Does . . . ?

What does a five hundred pound parrot say?

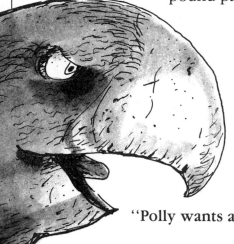

"Polly wants a cracker —
NOW!!!"

*Collected by Katie Krajina,
Vancouver, British Columbia.*

# What's in Your Lunchkit?

What's in your lunchkit?
Wagon wheels.

Can I have one please?
I forgot my lunch.
Er . . . no. I want them.

If I guess how many you've got,
can I have one?
Well . . . okay. If you guess right,
I'll give you both.

Gee — thanks! Okay. Is it three?

*Collected by Gail Fisher,
Whitehorse, Yukon.*

# What's Red and Goes Ding Dong?

What's red and goes ding dong?
Go on, guess.
Bet you can't. Bet you.
A fire engine.

Wrong. Two more guesses.
A Mickey Mouse telephone.

Wrong. One more guess.
Santa riding his sled.

Wrong. The answer's
a red ding dong, of course—
and that's a dollar you owe me.
One more chance. C'mon—just one.

Okay, okay: double or nothing.
What's blue and goes ding dong?
A blue ding dong.

What's green and goes ding dong?
A green ding dong.

What's white and goes ding dong?
A white ding dong.

Wrong, wrong, wrong!
They don't make them in that colour.
And that's *two* dollars you owe me.

*Marah Gilead*

# Doctor, Doctor

"Doctor, doctor, I keep thinking there's two of me."
"One at a time, please!"

"Doctor, doctor, I keeping thinking I'm a garbage can."
"Oh, don't talk such rubbish!"

"Doctor, doctor, I feel like a pack of cards."
"Wait and I'll deal with you later."

"Doctor, doctor, I keep thinking I'm a strawberry."
"Oh dear, you're really in a jam, aren't you!"

"Doctor, doctor, I feel like a pair of drapes."
"Well, pull yourself together then!"

"Doctor, doctor, I keep thinking I'm a clock."
"Well, don't get wound up about it."

"Doctor, doctor, I feel like a dollar bill."
"Go shopping, the change'll do you good."

"Doctor, doctor, everyone thinks I'm a liar."
"Really? I don't believe you!"

"Doctor, doctor, please will you help me out?"
"Sure. Which way did you come in?"

*Zoë Guimaldo*

# **Knock Knock.** Who's There?

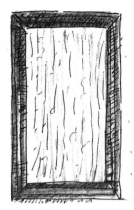  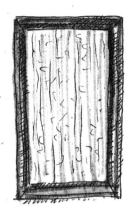

Des. **Des who?** Des no bell, dat's why I'm knocking.

Earl. **Earl who?** Earl be glad to tell you when you come to the door.

Emmett. **Emmett who?** Emmett the front door, not the back.

Howell. **Howell who?** Howell you know unless you come to the door?

Don. **Don who?** Don keep askin' — come find out for yourself.

Luke. **Luke who?** Luke through the keyhole and you'll see.

Max. **Max who?** Max no difference who's there — just open up.

Darius. **Darius who?** Darius a lot I want to talk to you about.

Dawn. **Dawn who?** Dawn keep me waiting.

Hyman. **Hyman who?** Hyman a terrible hurry.

Emma. **Emma who?** Emma getting to the end of my patience.

Betty. **Betty who?** Betty things to do than stand here answering questions.

Sacha. **Sacha who?** Sacha lot of questions you're asking.

Esther. **Esther who?** Esther any reason you don't come to the door?

Lisa. **Lisa who?** Lisa you can do is explain why you don't open up.

Ivor. **Ivor who?** Ivor open the door or I'll climb in the window.

Stan. **Stan who?** Stan back — I'm knocking the door down.

Xavier. **Xavier who?** Xavier breath, I'm coming down the chimney.

Ferdie. **Ferdie who?** Ferdie last time: o-p-e-n u-p!

Al. **Al who?** Al go home if you don't . . . I really will . . .

Olga. **Olga who?** Olga right now . . .

Elsie. **Elsie who?** Elsie you another day — *GOOD-BYE!*

*Meguido Zola*

Laughter, they say, is the best medicine. Laughter makes us feel good. And a good joke is the surest way to make us laugh. A good joke can lift our spirits and make us forget our troubles; it allows us to see the funny side of almost any situation. No wonder everyone loves to hear a good joke.

Jokes are not poetry—although some jokes may be poems. But jokes share some things in common with poetry. For that reason, they can help us understand something about poetry.

A poem, like a joke, is usually brief, simple, and to the point. A poem makes its point simply and directly. A poem may keep us thinking and feeling longer than it takes us to hear or read it.

Poems, like jokes, play with words in all kinds of ways.

Jokes have a kind of pattern. (Think of all the different patterns or *kinds* of jokes you know, e.g., knock, knock jokes and elephant jokes). And that's another thing poems have in common with jokes—patterns which come in all shapes and forms.

### 1. In a Small Group

- Take turns rereading the jokes in this Collection to each other. (Some of these jokes are written as if two people are talking. Read them that way.)
- Which jokes made you laugh the most? Why?
- Which jokes didn't make you laugh? Why?
- Did the way the jokes were told make any difference to your enjoyment of them? What difference did it make?
- On a large piece of paper, divided in half, make a list of all the things that make *Good Jokes* and *Not-So-Good-Jokes*.
- Share your thoughts with another group.

2. **With a Partner**  • Can you find the pattern in each joke in this Collection?
                        • Be ready to tell the class what you've found.

3. **With a Partner**  • Read "Knock, Knock. Who's There?"
                        • Take turns reading the questions and the answers. Read them as a chant. Make some "Knock, Knock" sounds to go with your reading.

4. **By Yourself**  • Make up some of your own "Knock, Knock" jokes.
                        • Make a booklet of all your "Knock, Knocks."
                        • Create a "Knock, Knock" cover.
                        • Hang your booklet on a "Knock, Knock" line.
                           P.S. Notice the *pattern* in "Knock, Knock" jokes?

5. **In a Small Group**  • Think of other kinds of jokes that have a strong pattern (such as "Waiter, Waiter" jokes, Tarzan jokes, canary jokes, etc.).
                        • Choose one of these pattern jokes and use it as a model for a joke poem of your own.
                        • Read your poem to another group. Can they help you make your poem funnier?
                        • Hang your finished poems on the "Joke Tree."

# MOUTH MUDDLERS, TEETH TANGLERS, and JAW JOSTLERS

**By Yourself**

- Can you say: "A noisy noise annoys an oyster"?
  And how fast can you say: "A big black bug bit a big black bear"?
  Or how many times can you say: "How high would a horsefly fly if a horsefly'd fly high?"

**With a Partner**

- Find some other mouth muddlers! Look in newspapers, magazines, and the telephone directory. Are there any you can think of in commercials?
- List them.
- Carefully print them on one long piece of paper.
- See how far down the list you and others can go without getting your tongues twisted.

*Note:* Read each list silently first.

Then read each list out loud as quickly as you can.

Becky Babcock

*Collected by Becky Babcock, North Vancouver, British Columbia*

Which is the witch that wished the wicked wish?

*Collected by Gail Fisher, Whitehorse, Yukon*

Mia mama me mime mucho.

*Collected by George Vallesquez, Prince Albert, Saskatchewan*

A tall girl named Short,
long loved a big Mr. Little.
But Little, thinking little of Short,
loved a little lass named Long.
To belittle Long, Short slyly said
*she* would marry Little before long.
This caused Little to shortly marry Long.

To make a long story short,
did tall Short love big Little less
because Little loved little Long more?

*Collected by Cami Watts,
Charlottetown, Prince Edward Island*

The skunk sat on a stump
and thunk the stump stunk
but the stump thunk
the skunk stunk

*Collected by Miki Zibarras,*
*Bathurst, New Brunswick*

Un chasseur
ne sachant pas chasser
sans son chien
est un mauvais chasseur

*Collected by Chloé Raunet,*
*Vancouver, British Columbia*

Betty Batter
bought some butter,
But, she said,
the butter's bitter.
If I put it
in my batter,
It will make
my batter bitter.
But a bit
of better butter—
THAT would make
my batter better.
So she bought
a bit of butter,
Better than
her bitter butter.
And she put it
in her batter,
And the batter
was not bitter.
So 'twas better
Betty Batter
Bought a bit
of better butter.

*Collected by Amanda Chalmers, Vancouver, B.C.*

Peter Piper picked a peck of pickled peppers.
Did Peter Piper pick a peck of pickled peppers?
If Peter Piper picked a peck of pickled peppers,
Where's the peck of pickled peppers Peter Piper picked?

*Collected by Wolfgang Hufnagel, Camrose, Alberta*

# Yellow Butter

Yellow butter purple jelly red jam black bread

Spread it thick
Say it quick

Yellow butter purple jelly red jam black bread

Spread it thicker
Say it quicker

Yellow butter purple jelly red jam black bread

Now repeat it
While you eat it

Yellow butter purple jelly red jam black bread

Don't talk
With your mouth full!

*Mary Ann Hoberman*

How many cans
Can a canner can
If a canner
Can can cans?
A canner can can
As many cans
As a canner can
If a canner
Can can cans.

*Collected by Joe Luterbach,*
*Toronto, Ontario*

## Sink Song

Scouring out the porridge pot,
    Round and round and round!

Out with all the scraith and scoopery,
Lift the eely ooly droopery,
Chase the glubbery slubbery gloopery
    Round and round and round!

Out with all the doleful dithery,
Ladle out the slimy slithery,
Hunt and catch the hithery thithery,
    Round and round and round!

Out with all the obbly gubbly,
On the stove it burns so bubbly,
Use the spoon and use it doubly,
    Round and round and round!

*J.A. Lindon*

You have just read a collection of *tongue twisters*. A tongue twister is a sequence of words that is difficult to say.

Tongue twisters, like poetry, are a kind of patterned language. And, like poetry, tongue twisters love words and delight in them, and play with them in all sorts of fun ways. Most of all, tongue twisters are like poetry in the way they play with (and can teach us to play with) the sound and rhythms and rhymes of language.

*1. By Yourself*

- Reread all of this Collection.
- Pick a short tongue twister, or part of a long one, that twists *your* tongue.
- Read it quietly to yourself many times; each time go a little faster. (Watch out! Your eyes might twist!)
- Copy this "twister" on a twisted tongue (*you* decide how to do that!) and be ready to say it to a partner.

*Note:* Tell us where your tongue twisted before you practised saying your twister aloud.

*2.   In a Small Group*

- Reread "Betty Batter," "Sink Song," or "Yellow Butter" silently.
- Decide who's going to say which lines of this tongue twister.
- Add some rhythm.
- Rehearse several times before presenting your choral reading to the class.

*Note:* You can add a few lines if you want!

| | |
|---|---|
| *3.* **With the Whole Class** | • Reread the poem about Peter Piper.<br>• Think about what makes the poem difficult to say. In tongue twisters, one or more sounds are repeated. This is called *alliteration*. Find other examples of alliteration in this Collection. |
| *4.a) By Yourself* | • Choose a consonant (e.g., f ), and list as many words as you can think of beginning with that letter (e.g., freckle, face, freak).<br>• Make up a sentence using some of your words (e.g., Freckle-faced Fred freaked Frankenstein).<br>• Add to the ideas in your twister to make up a longer twister. You might want to model it on one of the tongue twisters in the Collection. |
| *b) With a Partner* | • Read your tongue twisters to each other.<br>• Suggest to each other how you could make your twisters more twisted.<br>• Rewrite your twisters, and see how many tongues in the class you can twist! |
| *5.* **By Yourself** | • Collect several examples of tongue twisters from books, newspapers, magazines, or from friends or family members.<br>• Copy them down in rough.<br>• Make a good copy of your favourite and illustrate it. Put it in a class ''Mouth Muddlers, Teeth Tanglers, and Jaw Jostlers'' book.<br><br>*Note:* Be ready to say your favourite to the class. (Can anyone say it back to you?) |

**rhythm-n-rhyme-n-rhythm-n-rhyme-n-rhythm-n-
rhyme-n-rhythm-n-rhyme-n-rhythm-n-rhyme-n-
rhythm-n-rhyme-n-rhythm-n-rhyme-n-rhythm-n-
rhyme-n-rhythm-n-rhyme-n-rhythm-n-rhyme-n-**

# GETTING READY!

**In a Small Group**
- Write down two or three nursery rhymes that you remember.
- Say them together.
- Now, say the rhymes the same way you did when you were a little child.
- Add any actions you remember, or make up new ones.
- You might teach the rhymes to a group of very young children in your school. Encourage them to clap or beat out the rhythm.

**By Yourself**
- Write down your name.
- Write down some real and/or nonsense words that rhyme with your name.
- Make up a little poem or rhyme that's about you, using these words.

    *Note:* Be sure that your rhyme has rhythm . . . that the reader or listener could snap his or her fingers to the beat!

- Ask a partner to read your rhyme to you to see if it *sounds* right to you.

## Friendship Rhyme

Make friends, make friends,
Never, never break friends.

*Collected by Ulara Nakagawa,*
*North Vancouver, British Columbia*

## Taunts and Teases

Copy-catter, dirty ratter.

Tattle tale, ginger ale,
Stick your head in a garbage pail.

*Collected by Ajit Singh,*
*Halifax, Nova Scotia*

## Chants and Cheers

Two, four, six, eight,
who do we appreciate?
———, ———,
Yeah, yeah, ———.
1, 2, 3, 4, who are we for?
——, ——, ——, ——that's us!

*Collected by Anabel Alvarez,*
*Wawa, Ontario*

## Counting Out Rhymes

One-ery, two-ery, zickery, zan,
Hollow bone, crack a bone, nine-ery, ten;
Spinkum, spankum, winkum, wankum,
Twiddle-um, twaddle-um, twenty-one.

Johnson, Johnson,
Fly on your skateboard
You are in!
Drop a ballbearing
And you are out!

*Collected by Sean McLeod,*
*Lethbridge, Alberta*

# Skipping Rhymes

Strawberry slurpee, cream on top,
Tell me the name of my sweetheart
    A, B, C, D, E, ..............

Sales clerk, packer, disc jockey, cook,
Logger, golf pro, bookkeeper, crook;
Trucker, plumber, meatcutter, nurse,
Writer, welder, car wrecker, worse.

My mother owns a butcher shop,
My father cuts the meat,
And I am just their little kid,
Who runs across the street.
How many times do I cross?
1, 2, 3 . . .

*Collected by Cherie Plante,*
*Montreal, Quebec*

33

# The Fastest Train in the World

Tokyo to Kyoto
tokyotokyoto
kyotokyotokyotokyo
tokyotokyoto

*Keith Bosley*

# Turningwheelsturning

slow wheels
fast wheels
creaking-as-you-go wheels
speedy-as-the-wind wheels
clunk-clunk-clunk wheels

clicky wheels
quiet wheels
hands-over-your-ears wheels

round-another-bend wheels
up-another-hill wheels
swoosh-down-the-road wheels

STOP! RED LIGHT!

WHISTLE! WHISTLE!

GREEN LIGHT!

GO!

slow wheels
fast wheels
creak! . . . . . . . . .

*Emily Hearn*

# Toastertime

Tick tick tick tick tick tick tick
Toast up a sandwich quick quick quick
Hamwich
Jamwich
Lick lick lick!

Tick tick tick tick tick tick — stop!
    POP!

*Eve Merriam*

# The Washing Machine

It goes fwunkety,
   then slunkety,
as the washing goes around.

The water spluncheses,
   and it sluncheses,
as the washing goes around.

As you pick it out it splocheses,
   and it flocheses,
as the washing goes around,

But at the end it schlopperies,
   and then flopperies,
as the washing stops going around.

*Jeffrey Davies*

Poetry is not just something that poets write. If we listen closely enough, we can hear poetry all around us: in the sounds of our everyday world, in our everyday speech, in our games, and so on.

A good place for listening to this ''everyday'' poetry is on the school playground. Here, friendship rhymes, chants and cheers, taunts and teases, counting and skipping-rope rhymes are all part of schoolyard play. Some of these rhymes are sung, some are just spoken, and others are chanted — which is somewhere in between. Whatever way they're done, they help us understand something more about the sounds and rhythms and rhymes of poetry . . . and they lead us directly into some other exciting poetry of the everday world.

Rhythm is a regular beat that happens again and again. It runs through an everyday sound or movement or activity. (Can you think of examples?) Poems, too, have rhythms — you can hear them and you can feel them and, sometimes, you can see them.

Rhyme is the repetition of similar sounds. In a poem, the repetition usually comes at the end of a line. A poem doesn't have to rhyme to be a poem.

**1. In a Small Group**
- Read through the poems in this collection again.
- There is a particular rhythm or beat or movement in each poem. Identify it, describe it, talk about it — how successful is it and why? Which is your favourite?
- Does any poem show a strong connection between its rhythm and the subject or meaning of the poem? Which poem? How?
- Some words, such as *splash*, actually imitate or echo or suggest the sound of what they tell about. This is called *onomatopeia*.
- Find examples of onomatopeia in the poems in this Collection. Can you think of any examples of your own?
- Be ready to tell the rest of the class your answers.

**2. By Yourself**
- Ask your parents or your grandparents, or any older person, to tell you any rhymes they remember saying in the schoolyard when they were young.
- Ask them to tape-record the rhymes or write them out for you.
- Bring the rhymes into class for sharing.

**3. With a Partner or In a Small Group**
- Reread "Chants and Cheers."
- Then, ask a high school physical education teacher or student to tell you their school chant or cheer. Copy it down.
- *Think!* Make this chant come alive for the class. Practise it as if you were at a football or soccer game. Teach it to another group.

**4. By Yourself**
- Reread "The Fastest Train in the World," "Turningwheelsturning," "Toastertime," and "The Washing Machine."
  Think about a tool or appliance or machine that you use or are familiar with.
- What does it do? How do you use it? What does it sound like? How does it feel?
- Collect your ideas, and shape them into a poem.
- Make up some sound effects to go with your poem.
- Teach a partner how you want the poem to sound with the effects. Have your partner play the sounds while you say your poem!
- Rehearse the poem several times before presenting it to the class.

# WHAT'S THAT?

# GETTING READY!

**With a Partner**

- Read these riddles and guess the answers.

White as the clouds;
Yellow as the sun;
If I fall I break.
What am I?

A thousand legs
but
cannot walk
what am I?

A houseful, a roomful,
couldn't catch a cupful.
What is it?

(See page 128 for answers.)

**By Yourself**

- Make up a "What Am I?" riddle for which the answer is . . . a clock.
- Make up your own riddle and answer. Try it out on a partner.

**With a Partner**

- Think of two objects that could be the answer to a riddle.
- Write about both objects so that it's hard to tell what they are. (Don't name the objects!)
- Can other people in the class guess what the objects are?

## Holes

Why did the baker quit baking after all these years?

The more you take away from it, the bigger it gets. What is it?

*Collected by Jo Rigadelle, Regina, Saskatchewan*

## Out in the Field

Out in the field,
 there is a green house:
 inside that green house
 there is a white house;
 inside that white house
 there is a red house;
 and inside that red house
 there's a lot of . . .
 little white and black babies.

*Collected by Cami Watts,*
*Charlottetown, Prince Edward Island*

## It's Yours

It's yours and so belongs to you,
Yet others use it more than you.

*Collected by Pippa Emrick,*
*Vancouver, British Columbia*

## It's In

It's in the rock, but not in the stone;
It's in the marrow, but not in the bone;
It's in the mattress, but not in the bed;
It's not in the living, nor yet in the dead.

*Collected by Antoinette Keenleyside,*
*Fredericton, New Brunswick*

## Thirty White Horses

Thirty white horses
Upon a red hill:
Now they stamp,
Now they champ,
Now they stand still.

*Collected by Claudio Francescan,*
*Toronto, Ontario*

## It Has

It has: four step-standers
        four down hangers
        two lookers
        two crookers
        and a wig-wag
        swishy-wishy!
What is it?

*Collected by Cherie Plante,*
*Montreal, Quebec*

# A Room

A room with no walls,
A room with no doors,
A room with no floor.

*Collected by Melanie Boucher,*
*Burnaby, British Columbia*

# Two Legs . . .

Two legs sat upon three legs
with one leg in his lap.
In comes four legs
and runs away with one leg.
Up jumps two legs,
catches up three legs,
throws it after four legs,
and makes him bring back
one leg.

*Collected by Maryka Petrezen,*
*St. Boniface, Manitoba*

My dad's thumb
can stick pins in wood
without flinching—
it can crush family-size matchboxes
in one stroke
and lever off jam-jar lids without piercing
at the pierce here sign.

If it wanted
it could be a bath-plug
or a paint-scraper
a keyhole cover or a tap-tightener.

It's aleady a great nutcracker
and if it dressed up
it could easily pass
as a broad bean or a big toe.

In actual fact, it's quite simply
the world's fastest envelope burster.

*Michael Rosen*

# The Hardest Thing to Do in the World?

The hardest thing to do
in the world
is stand in the hot sun
at the end of a long queue for ice creams
watching all the people who've just bought theirs
coming away from the queue
giving their ice creams their very first lick

*Michael Rosen*

A black dot
a jelly tot

a water-wriggler
a tail jiggler

a cool kicker
a sitting slicker

a panting puffer
a fly-snuffer

a high-hopper
a belly-flopper

a catalogue
    to make me

FROG

*Libby Houston*

## Look

I eat from the dish of the world
    Trees, fields, flowers
I drink from the glass of space
    Blue sea, sky.
I pour the sky over me
    In blue showers
Look! I light up the day
    With my eye.

*John Smith*

"What walks on four legs early in the morning, on two legs during the day, and on three legs in the evening?"

That's one of the oldest riddles in the world. It used to be asked by the Sphinx of ancient Egypt. People who couldn't guess the answer were in real trouble!

The answer to the riddle, as you may or may not have guessed, is people. People crawl early in life; walk through most of life; and, late in life, may need a cane to help them walk.

Riddles share much with poetry; and so riddles tell us a lot about poetry.

Like a riddle, a poem creates pictures with words in a special way. It describes ordinary things in extraordinary ways.

Like a riddle, a poem is a special way of looking at the world. It helps us to understand and appreciate the world better.

**1. In a Small Group**
- Make up a chart like the one opposite.
- Reread the riddles listed in the chart.
- Write down your guess to each riddle.
- Be ready to show the rest of the class your chart and to tell why you chose your answers.

### What's That?

| Riddle | Our Guess | Other Answers |
|---|---|---|
| Holes | | |
| It's Yours | | |
| It's In | | |
| Out in the Field | | |
| Thirty White Horses | | |
| It Has | | |
| A Room | | |
| Two Legs | | |
| Look | | |

**2. With the Whole Class**
- Listen to other groups' guesses.
- Add their answers to your chart.

**3. With a Partner**
- Collect other riddles or riddle poems. Be ready to ask the class to solve some of your riddles.

**4. With a Partner or By Yourself**
- Make a collection of riddles that have one theme (e.g., riddles about people, elephant riddles, etc.).
- Shape your riddles into some pattern so that the collection is like a kind of poem. You might make it rhyme, make it have a beat or rhythm; and you might sequence it like a story, or like a play.
- Illustrate your collection.

**By Yourself**
- Reread "My Dad's Thumb."
- Think of another object that does lots of jobs, and think about what else it could do.
- Make a list of ideas and shape them into a poem modelled on "My Dad's Thumb."

**In a Small Group**
- Share your poems with each other.
- Can you think of other ideas to add to each other's poems?

# PICTURES IN MY HEAD

# *GETTING READY!*

*By Yourself*

- If you can, find somewhere to be alone; or close your eyes so you feel alone.
- Give yourself time. Picture these things one at a time:
  You are . . . somewhere really hot (or icy cold)
  . . . in a situation where your life is in
  danger
  . . . somewhere strange and unusual
- Now, sketch or write about one of these scenes. Remember as much detail as possible.

*With a Partner*

- Take turns doing this:
  1. One person (A) closes his or her eyes.
  2. The other person (B) chooses one of the following scenes (or makes one up) and tells it to A.
     - in an old, abandoned house
     - on horseback
     - running down a hill
     - inside the belly of a whale
     - riding a giraffe
     - cutting down a tree
     - rolling in maple syrup
  3. A tells B all the things she/he sees.
  4. B writes down these details as quickly as they're spoken.
- Repeat as often as you wish.
- Then, choose the most interesting list and read it to each other. Make it sound like a poem.

## Cartwheels

spread out your legs
that stand on grass

spread out your arms
that reach to sky

your stretching body
an X
uniting the elements

spring
and turn
sideways

spreading your arms
that touch on grass

spreading your legs
that reach to sky

arms and legs
whirling spokes
in wheels of air

spin! spin!
X's O's

noughts and crosses
tic tac toe
hugs and kisses
of love and
freedom
whirling in
ecstasies
of space

cartwheels
turning
turn
tu

collapse
in a crumple
of thumps
and giggles
and sticking-out
limbs

spokes uneven
circle misshapen

faulty wheel

grounded

*Emily Hearn*

## Summer

When it's hot
I take my shoes off,
I take my shirt off,
I take my pants off,
I take my underwear off,
I take my whole body off,
and throw it
in the river.

*Frank Asch*

## Saturday's Bath

a drum of rain water
cascades,
cold, glassy,
breath catches
leaving gasps,
sprouting pores,
shocking skin,
bringing tears.

*Dionne Brand*

## Zebra

white sun
black
fire escape,

morning
grazing like a zebra
outside my window.

*Judith Thurman*

## Rain

Rain drums on the pane

    and runs down, wavering the world

        into a dream.

*J. W. Hackett*

## Jigsaw Puddle

Sloshing my boot in the pavement puddle
I jiggle the sky above,

I fold the clouds in a sheep-like huddle,
I bobble the sun in the blue and white muddle—

And then I stand still—

Till the jigsaw puddle
Is smooth as a mirror again!

*Emily Hearn*

# Passing by the Junkyard

Heaps of headlights
    stare
    at me.

radiators, wheels
    and
    fan-belts
    smile.

And a thousand
    more parts—
    rusty and new,

Seem to say
    they'd all like
    to go
    on a
    car-ride
    again.

*Charles J. Egita*

# The Toaster

A silver-scaled Dragon with jaws flaming red
Sits at my elbow and toasts my bread.
I hand him fat slices, and then, one by one,
He hands them back when he sees they are
done.

*William Jay Smith*

# The Garden Hose

In the grey evening
I see a long green serpent
With its tail in the dahlias.

It lies in loops across the grass
And drinks softly at the faucet.

I can hear it swallow.

*Beatrice Janosco*

Poems create pictures inside your head. But, instead of using paint and brushes or cameras, poems use words. And these pictures in your head, or *images*, are not on canvas or on film but inside you.

You may see exactly what the poet saw and wanted you to see . . . or you may have a picture that's different from what anyone else can see. And that's the beauty of poetry!

The exciting thing is that, after you've put the poem away, the picture stays in your mind.

1. **With a Partner or In a Small Group**

You learn about the world around you through your five senses: sight, hearing, touch, taste, and smell. You make use of these senses all the time to interact with your world. The poems in this collection focus on the use of the senses.

- Reread the poems in this Collection.
- What senses does each of the poems appeal to?
- Which poem makes the best picture in your head? How does it do this?
- Start a "Big Book of Sense Poems." Find other poems to add to your book. Be ready to share them with another group.

2. **By Yourself**

- Reread "Cartwheels," "Summer," and "Saturday's Bath." Think about something you do often or every day (e.g., brushing your teeth, eating your recess snack, etc.)
- Think about and recall one or more times you have done this thing; while you are doing this thing, you are using your senses—sight, hearing, touch, smell, taste.
- Think of the words and phrases and sentences that help you express what you can see, hear, touch, smell, and taste.
- Shape these words into a poem that is similar to "Cartwheels" or "Summer" or "Saturday's Bath."

| | |
|---|---|
| 3. **In a Small Group** | Some of these poems use images that are likenesses or comparisons. The poets have put together things in new or unusual or surprising ways.<br>• What is likened or compared to what in each of "Zebra," "The Toaster," "Passing By the Junkyard," and "The Garden Hose"?<br>• What do you think of these likenesses or comparisons? |
| 4. **With a Partner** | • Reread "Passing by the Junkyard," "The Toaster," and "The Garden Hose." These poems describe everyday objects. But the poets see these objects in new or unexpected ways: the toaster becomes a dragon, the junkyard items stare and smile and talk, and so on.<br>• Think about an object you are very familiar with and/or use on a regular basis (e.g., a ruler, a TV).<br>• What does this object remind you of? What is it like? What could you compare It with? Think of various possibilities. Choose one.<br>• Brainstorm some pictures that come to your mind; list them, play with them on paper.<br>• Shape your likenesses or comparison into a poem.<br>• Share your poem with another group. |
| 5.a) **By Yourself** | • Make a list of some sounds you like or dislike. ("Summer" is a kind of list: a list of items that the poet takes off and throws in the river to cool off when he is hot.)<br>• Revise your list to give it some kind of pattern—any kind of pattern (e.g., from softest to loudest sounds, or sounds that surprise or scare you, or sounds that keep you awake at night, etc.)<br>• Shape your list into a poem. |
| b) **With a Partner** | • Share your poem with a partner. Discuss it: are there ways you can improve your poem—make it clearer, more interesting, more powerful? Revise it. Share your poem with a new partner. |

# INSIDE ME!

# GETTING READY!

**With a Partner**

- Have your partner trace the outline of your body (lying flat? running?).
- If the weather's good, and you have permission, do this outside, first, with chalk. Then, do it on a large sheet of mural paper.

**By Yourself**

- Fill the outline of your body shape with words and pictures (sketches? photos? magazine cuttings?) of all the things that you do, you feel, you eat, you dream. Show it to others in the class to see if they can see all the things that are inside you.
- Display your shape poem!

## Where

Where
Have you been dear?
What
Have you seen dear?
What
Did you do there?
Who
Went with you there?
Tell me
What's new dear?
What's
New with you dear?
Where
Will you go next?
What
Will you do?

"I do this and I do that.
I go here and I go there.
At times I like to be alone.
There are some thoughts that are my own
I do not wish to share."

*Karla Kuskin*

## Sometimes

Sometimes I share things,
And everyone says
"Isn't it lovely? Isn't it fine?"

I give my little brother
Half my ice-cream cone
And let him play
With toys that are mine.

But today
I don't feel like sharing.
Today
I want to be let alone.
Today
I don't want to give my little brother
A single thing except
A shove.

*Eve Merriam*

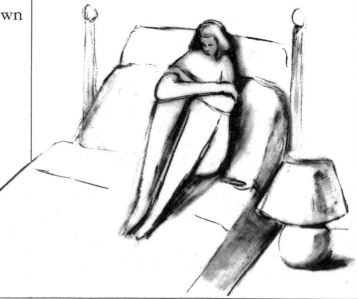

# Leave Me Alone

Loving care!
Too much to bear.
**Leave me alone!**

Don't brush my hair,
Don't pat my head,
Don't tuck me in
Tonight in bed,
Don't ask me if I want a sweet,
Don't fix my favorite things to eat,
Don't give me lots of good advice,
And most of all just don't be nice.

But when I've wallowed well in sorrow,
Be nice to me again tomorrow.

*Felice Holman*

# Tempers

Boy, when Woody's mad
He can really roar.
I don't know, but I suppose
They hear me through the door,
Too.

*Mary Neville*

# Wicked Thoughts

The meanest girl I've ever met
Is Mary Ellen Wright,
And if a lion came along and
Ate her with one bite,
I'd cry and cry and cry and cry.
(But just to be polite)

## More Wicked Thoughts

Jennifer Jill has the brainiest of all the brains
    in class.
Jennifer Jill has the prettiest of faces.
Jennifer Jill has a real gold watch and ten best friends
    and the leading role in the Christmas play.
(I'm glad that Jennifer Jill has to wear braces.)

## And Some More Wicked Thoughts

In every race I've ever run
I'm number two; Joe's number one.
There's awful things that I could do
To make me one and make Joe two.
(But I won't even think of them).

*Judith Viorst*

# Habits

Whenever I smile
I cover my mouth
With my hand.

When I was six
I had three bad front teeth:
That's when
I learned
To cover my mouth.

I guess
Habits
Last longer
Than cavities.
You see,
A good dentist
Gave me Pepsodent whites . . .
But my hand
Doesn't believe it.

*Carolyn Mamchur*

# Inside Me

Inside me
is another
Jo Lena:

who doesn't
stammer when
she gets
embarrassed;

who doesn't
refuse
chocolate cake
when she
really wants
a piece;

who doesn't
make up lies
in front of
the gang
in order
to be noticed;

and who's
never even
heard of
Remedial
Reading
Clinic.

*Jo Lena*

# Courage

Courage is when you're
allergic to cats and
your new friend says can
you come to her house to
play after school and
stay to dinner then
maybe go skating and
sleep overnight. And,
she adds, you can pet
her small kittens. Oh,
how you ache to. It
takes courage to
say 'no' to all that.

*Emily Hearn*

You are unique! You are special! And you are human—not a machine or a robot. You laugh, cry, hurt, fear, hunger, worry, giggle, dream . . . But most of all . . . *you feel*!

The poems in this collection remind us about feelings. A poem shares feelings with us and, in turn, makes us feel things as we hear or read it.

*1. By Yourself*

- Read the collection again, to yourself.
- Which poem tells about feelings inside *you*?

*2. In a Small Group*

- Take turns reading a different poem out loud to the rest of the group.
- Experiment with different ways of presenting the poem; for instance, "Where" can be read in two parts—questioner and respondent. "Leave Me Alone" can be read in several parts. "Wicked Thoughts" can be acted out in three parts, since it's a trilogy (three separate poems in one).
- After you've dramatized two or three of these poems, use music and props to present one to the rest of the class.

*3. By Yourself*

- Reread the "Wicked Thoughts" trilogy.
- Why do people have wicked thoughts? Do you think wicked thoughts are harmful? Sometimes? Always? Never? Explain your answer.
- Privately, jot down some of your own wicked thoughts and why you have them. Keep your list.
- Now, share one of your wicked thoughts if you are comfortable doing so.
- Use your "wicked thoughts" list to make a comic strip. Show your characters saying polite things while thinking "wicked thoughts."

**4. By Yourself**

- Write about "The Me Nobody Knows . . ." Describe the person you know that is inside you but that many people may not recognize as being like you. For example, if people say you are the shy, quiet type, they may not know the exciting imagination and longing for adventure that is a very real part of your personality. Write about that.

**5. With a Small Group**

- Read "Where."
- What might be some of our reasons for wanting to keep our thoughts private?
- How do you feel when you are bombarded with questions about these thoughts? Talk about these things.
- Appoint a group secretary to record the following information on recipe cards:
  — how you feel when asked these questions
  — how you usually answer these questions
  — what you really think or feel or wish you'd said.
- When you have filled approximately 10–12 recipe cards, have the secretary of the group read them aloud. Now, as a group, write a poem using this model:

  > When they ask . . .
  > I answer . . .
  > And I reply . . .
  > But I really think . . .

**6. By Yourself**

- Reread "Leave Me Alone."
- Do you ever just want to be left alone?
- What sorts of things do people do that bother you at times? Jot them down and use your list to complete the following poem.

  > Sometimes I just want to be left alone.
  > Don't _____
  > Or _____
  > Or _____
  > And especially don't _____
  > Please, just leave me alone.

- Now, rewrite the poem using "do" instead of "don't."

# QUESTIONS!
# QUESTIONS!
# QUESTIONS!

# GETTING READY!

**By Yourself**
- Divide a large sheet of paper into six parts.
- Write one of these words in the middle of each part. Who? What? Where? When? Why? and How?
- Write down at least three questions for each word: you may or may not know the answers!

**With a Partner or In a Small Group**
- Add to each other's list of questions.
- Make one giant flowchart of all your questions.
- Make a similar chart that has some or all of the answers on it.

Find another group or set of partners and share your questions
- Can someone offer some different answers?
- Can you change the *shape* of your flowchart so you have a poem?

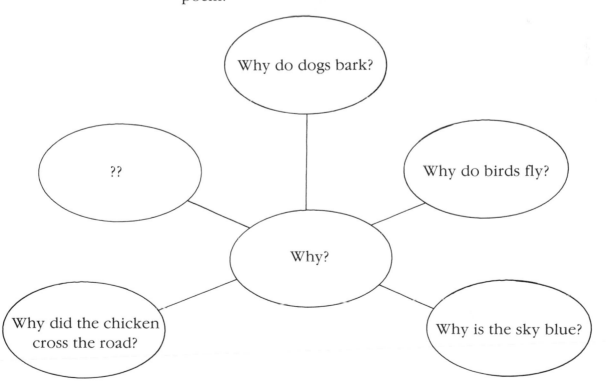

# Dog, Where Did You Get That Bark?

Dog, where did you get that bark?
Dragon, where did you get that flame?
Kitten, where did you get that meow?
Rose, where did you get that red?
Bird, where did you get those wings?

*Desiree Lynne Collier*

# Horrible Things

''What's the horriblest thing you've seen?''
Said Nell to Jean.

''Some grey-coloured, trodden-on plasticine;
On a plate, a left-over cold baked bean;
A cloak-room ticket numbered thirteen;
A slice of meat without any lean;
The smile of a spiteful fairy-tale queen;
A thing in the sea like a brown submarine;
A cheese fur-coated in brilliant green;
A bluebottle perched on a piece of sardine.
What's the horriblest thing *you've* seen?''
Said Jean to Nell.

''Your face, as you tell
Of all the horriblest things you've seen.''

*Roy Fuller*

# Zebra Question

I asked the zebra,
Are you black with white stripes?
Or white with black stripes?
And the zebra asked me,
Are you good with bad habits?
Or are you bad with good habits?
Are you noisy with quiet times?
Or are you quiet with noisy times?
Are you happy with some sad days?
Or are you sad with some happy days?
Are you neat with some sloppy ways?
Or are you sloppy with some neat ways?
And on and on and on and on
And on and on he went.
I'll never ask a zebra
About stripes
Again.

*Shel Silverstein*

# Some Things Don't Make Any Sense At All

My mom says I'm her sugarplum.
My mom says I'm her lamb.
My mom says I'm completely perfect
Just the way I am.
My mom says I'm a super-special wonderful terrific
    little guy.
My mom just had another baby.
Why?

*Judith Viorst*

# Glenis

The teacher says:

Why is it, Glenis,
Please answer me this,
The only time
You ever stop talking in class
Is if I ask you
Where's the Khyber Pass?
Or when was the Battle of Waterloo?
Or what is nine times three?
Or how do you spell
Mississippi?
Why is it, Glenis,
The only time you are silent
Is when I ask you a question?

And Glenis says:


*Allan Ahlberg*

# Art

Why do some people
Ask you
What is it?
Sometimes
Woody and I
Just like to paint
Nothin'.

*Mary Neville*

## Just When . . .

Just when they're watching TV
and I'm ready for bed,
the hardest questions
pop into my head.
It might make them angry,
but I really can't wait
'cause "later"
is always too late.

*Jehuda Atlas*

## Seems I'm Never
## Old Enough

Seems I'm never old enough,
to know the secrets
grown-ups share.
You wouldn't understand,
they say.
But when I'm wrong,
you hear them shout,
Girl, you should have known!

*Nikki Grimes*

Questions, questions! The world seems full of questions.

Some questions are fun—like riddles, and knock, knock jokes, and guessing games.

Some questions are perfectly reasonable: How old are you? How do you make a peanut butter and jelly sandwich?

Some questions are silly: What noise annoys an oyster? How much wood would a woodchuck chuck if a woodchuck could chuck wood?

Often, a poem is meant to leave us with a question. And maybe there's an answer, maybe there isn't.

Then there are those questions that aren't even meant to be answered. If someone asks, "How many times do I have to tell you . . ." What do you suppose would happen if you said, "Eighty-seven"?

1. *By Yourself*
- Reread all the poems in this Collection.
- Choose the poem that asks the most interesting question.
- Write down the question on one side of a piece of paper. On the other side, show the answer . . . in an illustration, in a list, or in a poem.

  *P.S.* Take a guess at the answer if you're not sure!

- Exchange pieces of paper with a partner. Do you agree with each other's answers? Tell your partner why or why not.

2. *With a Partner*
- Reread "Dog, Where Did You Get That Bark?" The answers seem to be simple, but really, they're quite tricky!
- What does the poem say to you?
- Think of similar questions that are tricky to answer.
- Shape them into a poem modelled on "Dog, Where Did You Get That Bark?"

| | |
|---|---|
| *3.* **In a Small Group** | • Reread ''Glenis'' and ''Art.'' |
| | • Now think! What do you feel are the most difficult questions to answer in school? Think back to times when you have found it difficult to answer a question: Why was it difficult? How did you feel? |
| | • Are you ever asked questions which you can answer but which, for some reason, you don't want to answer? When might this happen? Why? What do you do? |
| | • Make a list of these questions. |
| | • Choose the best ideas that your group has come up with and arrange them in a list called ''Please Don't Ask . . . .'' |
| *4.a)* **In a Small Group** | • Reread ''Seems I'm Never Old Enough'' and ''Just When . . . .'' |
| | • Have you ever been in the kind of situations described in these two poems? What did you do? How did you feel? |
| | • Why do you think adults behave this way? |
| *b)* **By Yourself** | • Make a list of some of the things it seems you are never old enough to know. |
| | • Now, make a list of the grown-up things you are expected to know. |
| | • Using these two lists, create a poem entitled ''You Just Can't Win.'' You might use the following repetitive pattern — or something like it. |

I'm too young to _____,
But I'm not old enough to _____,

• Share your poem with a partner. Suggest one or two ways in which you could improve your poems. Revise your poems carefully, and make a good copy.

# EATS
# TREATS
# EATS
# TREATS
# EATS
# TREATS

# GETTING READY!

Are you always hungry?
Is your stomach a bottomless pit?
Do you have a hollow leg?
If so, this collection of "Eats" is especially for you.
If not, join in the fun anyway.
*Warning:* Not to be read if there's too long to wait for recess or lunchtime!

*With a Partner*
- Collect or draw pictures of your favourite food.
- Under each picture, write down several words that describe that food.
- Choose one picture and, using the words you have listed, make up a commercial for the food.
- Present your commercial to another set of partners.

*By Yourself*
- Begin to collect wrappers, cartons, labels, etc. of food you eat. Save them in a big garbage bag that has your name on it.

## eats

are on my mind from early morning
    to late at night
           in spring
           or winter
  there is
    no wrong
    or right
     time
    to feel that sudden
         need
    to find that sudden
         meal

  i am always hungry

*Arnold Adoff*

## not me but

cows walk up and beg to
              be
          burgers
chicken legs
    will tap dance
            to
           my
      teeth
and
oatmeal cookies
    have
    been
      known
to fly
  out of their jars
  as I pass by

*Arnold Adoff*

## my mouth

stays shut
     but
food just
finds
   a way
      my tongue says
we are
    full today
    but
       teeth just
        grin
  and
  say
    come in

I am always hungry

*Arnold Adoff*

## One Hamburger, Please

Hamburger
with everything?

Yes — but without . . .
     mustard
     relish
     ketchup
     bacon
     mayonnaise
     tomato
     lettuce
     onions
     pickle
     cheese . . .
     One *plain* hamburger.

*Meguido Zola*

## Six Things Not to Put in My Lunchbox

carrots
celery sticks
tuna fish sandwich
pickles
smelly cheese
grape–flavour anything

*Jay Paul Booth*

# Here We Go Lobster Loo

I went to a very expensive
Restaurant
With my Mother (from Halifax)
She said to have lobster
Melt-in-the-mouth lobster
But she didn't tell me
Lobster's alive,
All green and crawling
In an old aquarium.

I choose the saddest one.
They boiled him alive.
ALIVE.
I listened to my plate. No sound.

Then I took the pliers
And cracked and crushed
And scraped the pink flesh
Into my red mouth.

I told her I loved lobster.
But they belong in Nova Scotia
With my grandfather,
Not on my fork.

*David Booth*

# When They Give Me...

When they give me chili
I want hamburger and chips.
When they give me hamburger and chips
I want hot dog.
When they give me hot dog
I want fish sticks and rice.

But when they give me macaroni and cheese
I want macaroni and cheese—
**Right now**, please!

*Marah Gilead*

# Garbage Delight

Now, I'm not the one
To say No to a bun,
And I always can manage some jelly;
If somebody gurgles,
"Please try my hamburgles,"
I try to make room in my belly.
I seem, if they scream,
Not to gag on ice-cream,
And with fudge I can choke down my fright;
But none is enticing
Or even worth slicing,
Compared with Garbage Delight.

With nip and a nibble
A drip and a dribble
A dollop, a walloping bite:
If you want to see grins
All the way to my shins,
Then give me some Garbage Delight!

I'm handy with candy.
I star with a bar.
And I'm known for my butterscotch burp;
I can stare in the eyes
Of a Toffee Surprise
And polish it off with one slurp.
My lick is the longest,
My chomp is the champ
And everyone envies my bite;
But my talents were wasted
Until I had tasted
The wonders of Garbage Delight.

With nip and a nibble
A drip and a dribble
A dollop, a walloping bite:
If you want to see grins
All the way to my shins,
Then give me some Garbage Delight!
  Right now!
Please pass me the Garbage Delight!

*Dennis Lee*

Everybody loves food (though not everybody likes the same kind of food). Often, people choose to eat a particular food because of the way it's presented. TV commercials and magazine ads make food look so good, you can almost taste it. A hamburger patty looks thick and juicy; the bun is fresh and soft; the lettuce and tomato topping look mouth-wateringly crisp. And the pickles, relish, and ketchup just can't be missed. You can almost taste that hamburger.

Could you taste the foods described in this Collection?

1. **By Yourself**
   - Take the time to reread all the poems.
   - Try not to lick your lips!

2. **In a Small Group**
   - Each of you select an "Eats" poem you like. Practise reading it aloud, by yourself first. Now read the poem aloud to the group. Applaud each performance!

3. a) **By Yourself**
   - Think about an eating experience that really stands out in your memory. It might be amusing, embarrassing, mouth-watering, or sickening.
   - Where did it happen? When? Why? Who else was there?
   - Tell your experience to a partner.

   b) **With a Partner or In a Small Group**
   - Choose one experience to make into a very short play. Put in lots of details to make sure your audience *feels* what you felt!

4. **With a Partner or In a Small Group**
   - Find several other food poems.
   - Create a menu to go with your poems.
   - Copy your poems and menu onto chart paper.

5. **By Yourself**
   Eating can be fun. Think of a favourite food: think about it exactly; imagine yourself eating it.
   - What does it look like?
   - How does it taste? How does it feel? How does it smell?

- Do you eat it with a fork? Your tongue? Your hands?
- How do you go about eating it? Slowly? Quickly?
- How do you eat the last bite?
- Could you share it?

Collect the answers to some of these and other questions into a poem. Be sure to write mostly things that are very real: things that your reader can see or taste or smell or feel. You might end your poem with
"Eating _____ is (like) _____."

6. **With a Partner**
- Reread "Here We Go Lobster Loo."
- How does the boy feel about eating lobster? Why?
- After reading this poem, would *you* like to eat lobster?
- What details in the poem make you feel the way you do?

7. **By Yourself**
- Reread "Six Things Not to Put in My Lunchbox" and "One Hamburger, Please." Think about a food that you don't like to eat. Think about why you don't like to eat it. Maybe it comes from an animal that you're especially fond of. Maybe it just *looks* awful.
- Write a poem about this food. Try to persuade your readers not to eat it. You'll do this best by creating a picture for your readers. Put in as many facts as you can—just as Booth has done in "Here We Go Lobster Loo."

8. **In a Small Group**
- Read your poem out loud. Ask your classmates how they felt when you were reading it. Ask them which part worked best for them.
- Rewrite your poem, taking out parts that didn't work and improving those that did.

9. **By Yourself**
- Glue or tape together the wrappers, cartons, labels, etc. you've collected in your garbage bag.
- Make a "Garbage Delight" sculpture!
- Reread "Garbage Delight" while building your sculpture.
- Glue or paint words on your sculpture to make it into a 3-D poem!

# GETTING INTO MISCHIEF

***By Yourself***

- Have you ever been caught in the act of doing something that you knew wasn't bad, but that you also knew you shouldn't be doing and didn't want to get caught doing?
- What happened? How did it feel while you were doing it? How did it feel when you got caught? (or when you didn't get caught and got away with it?)
- Write down your feelings.

***With a Partner***

- Think of a person or an animal you have known or read about who is always getting into mischief. (Or, perhaps, invent one.)
- Think of a story, or make one up of your own, in which this person or animal gets into mischief.
- Present your story in a cartoon strip. Show what your character is thinking and feeling.

## Chocolate Cake

I love chocolate cake.
And when I was a boy
I loved it even more.

Sometimes we used to have it for tea
and Mum used to say,
"If there's any left over
you can have it to take to school
tomorrow to have at playtime."
And the next day I would take it to school
wrapped up in tin foil
open it up at playtime and sit in the
corner of the playground
eating it;
you know how the icing on top
is all shiny and it cracks as you
bite into it
and there's that other kind of icing in
the middle
and it sticks to your hands and you
can lick your fingers
and lick your lips
oh it's lovely.
Yeah.

Anyway,
once we had this chocolate cake for tea
and later I went to bed
but while I was in bed
I found myself waking up
licking my lips
and smiling.
I woke up proper.
"The chocolate cake."
It was the first thing
I thought of.
I could almost see it
so I thought,
what if I go downstairs
and have a little nibble, yeah?

It was all dark
everyone was in bed
so it must have been really late
but I got out of bed,
crept out of the door

there's always a creaky floorboard,
isn't there?

80

Past Mum and Dad's room,

careful not to tread on bits of broken toys
or bits of Lego
you know what it's like treading on Lego
with your bare feet,

yowwww
shhhhhh

downstairs
into the kitchen
open the cupboard
and there it is
all shining.

So I take it out of the cupboard
put it on the table
and I see that
there's a few crumbs lying about on the plate,
so I lick my finger and run my finger all over
the crumbs
scooping them up
and put them into my mouth.

ooooooommmmmmmm

nice.

Then
I look again
and on one side where it's been cut,
it's all crumbly.
So I take a knife
I think I'll just tidy that up a bit,
cut off the crumbly bits
scoop them all up
and into the mouth

oooooommm   mmmmm.
nice.

Look at the cake again.

That looks a bit funny now,
one side doesn't match the other
I'll just even it up a bit, eh?

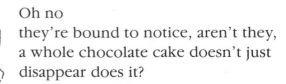

Take the knife
and slice.
This time the knife makes a little cracky noise
as it goes through that hard icing on top.

A whole slice this time,

into the mouth.

Oh the icing on top
and the icing in the middle
ohhhhhh oooo mmmmmm.

But now
I can't stop myself.
Knife—
I just take any old slice at it
and I've got this great big chunk
and I'm cramming it in
what a greedy pig
but it's so nice,

and there's another
and another and I'm squealing and I'm
    smacking my lips
and I'm stuffing myself with it
and
before I know
I've eaten the lot.

The whole lot.
I look at the plate.
It's all gone.

Oh no
they're bound to notice, aren't they,
a whole chocolate cake doesn't just
disappear does it?

What shall I do?

I know. I'll wash the plate up,
and the knife

and put them away and maybe no one
**will** notice, eh?

So I do that
and creep creep creep
back to bed
into bed
doze off
licking my lips
with a lovely feeling in my belly.
Mmmmmmmmmmm.

In the morning I get up,
downstairs,
have breakfast.
Mum's saying,
"Have you got your dinner money?"
and I say,
"Yes"
"And don't forget to take some chocolate
    cake with you."
I stopped breathing.

"What's the matter," she says,
"you normally jump at chocolate cake?"

I'm still not breathing,
and she's looking at me very closely now.
She's looking at me just below my mouth.
"What's that?" she says.
"What's what?" I say.
"What's that there?"
"Where?"
"There," she says, pointing to my chin.
"I don't know," I say.
"It looks like chocolate," she says.
"It's not chocolate cake is it?"
No answer.
"Is it?"
"I don't know."
She goes to the cupboard
looks in, up, top, middle, bottom,
turns back to me.
"It's gone.
It's gone.
You haven't eaten it, have you?"
"I don't know."
"You don't know? You don't know if you've
eaten a whole chocolate cake or not?
When? When did you eat it?"

So I told her,

and she said
well what could she say?
"That's the last time I give you any cake to
take to school.
Now go. Get out
no wait
not before you've washed your dirty sticky
face."
I went upstairs
looked in the mirror
and there it was,
just below my mouth,
a chocolate smudge.
The give-away.
Maybe she'll forget about it by next week.

*Michael Rosen*

Have you ever noticed how grownups talk about kids getting into mischief as though it were something kids did on purpose? Doesn't mischief just happen . . . ?

Ten-year-old Cari Robertson of Langley, British Columbia, explains it this way: "Getting into mischief is usually something you don't know you're doing at the time—at least, you *sort* of know, but you sort of *don't* know. It just kind of happens . . . Then, maybe, you suddenly realize what you've done—but by then it's too late!

"Or, at other times, it's just that you've done something that starts one way but turns out another way—not at all as you'd planned or anticipated . . .

"Or, sometimes, it's that you've done something that someone else disapproves of. That gets called getting into mischief, too."

Whichever way you look at it, everyone—even grownups—gets into mischief at one time or another.

1. *In a Small Group*

- Reread "Chocolate Cake." As you read, see if you can imagine what is happening as if you were watching the events on a movie screen. Can you do this better with some parts? Which ones? Why?
- Talk about the story that is told in this poem.
- Fold a large sheet of paper in half. On the left-hand side, write down the events of the story in the order in which they happened.
- On the right-hand side, write down how the boy felt as each event happened.
- Discuss your findings.

**2.a) With a Partner**
- Think of times when you were caught getting into mischief.
- Now, choose one of these incidents and tell your partner exactly what happened, as you remember it:
- Choose a story you get excited about while you're telling it. Do you feel like blushing or squirming or laughing while you're telling it? If so, you have probably found the right story for telling.
- Tell all the events that form part of your story.
- Make sure you talk about your feelings at the time.

**b) By Yourself**
- Write down the story you told your partner. Write it as a story or as a poem.
- Check to make sure that you've included all the details and all of your feelings.

**c) With a Partner**
- Take turns reading your stories or poems to each other. (Work with the same partner as before.)
- Tell each other which parts of the story you can picture and which you can't.
- Ask each other what you think each other felt.
- Revise your stories or poems.

**d) With a Partner or In a Small Group**
- Act out one another's stories or poems. Take the story or poem, read it to yourself and, without using a script, act it out to the group. You may use words if you want to, or you may just mime the story. The major events in the story should be clear from your acting it out.
- Do some parts have to be added or deleted to make the story work?

**3. By Yourself**
- Often parents and grandparents enjoy telling about times in their past when they got into mischief. It might be fun to interview an adult you know who has a mischief story to tell. Record one such story and make a story poem of it to give back to the teller as a present.

# BEDTIME

**By Yourself**

You've finished your dinner. You've finished playing with your friends. You've finished watching TV. You've finished reading. It's bedtime.

- Make a list of all the things you do to get ready for bed. Really *think*! Put every little detail on the list.
- The last thing on your list should be "Z-z-z-z-z-z-z, which is *you* . . . falling asleep.
- Take a close look at your list.
- Write it up on a long sheet of paper as a bedtime poem.
- What are you going to call your poem?

**In a Small Group**

- Read each other's "Bedtime" poems.
- Put them together in a booklet.
- Add illustrations.

# Last One Into Bed

''Last one into bed
has to switch out the light.''
It's just the same every night.
There's a race.
I'm ripping off my trousers and shirt—
he's kicking off his shoes and socks.

''My sleeve's stuck.''
''This button's too big for its button-hole.''
''Have you hidden my pyjamas?''
''Keep your hands off mine.''
If you win
you get where it's safe
before the darkness comes—
but if you lose
if you're last:
you know what you've got coming up is
the journey from the light switch
to your bed.
It's the Longest Journey in the World.

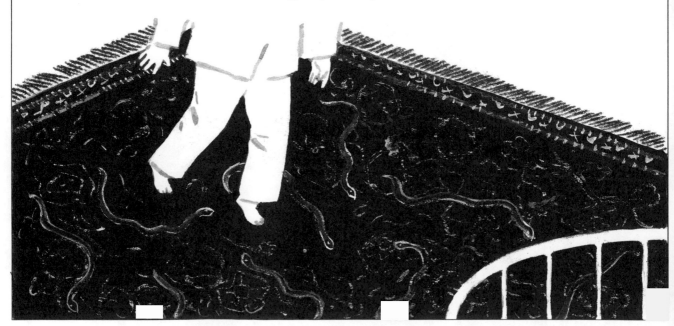

"You're last tonight," my brother says.
And he's right.
There is nowhere so dark
as that room in the moment
after I've switched out the light.

There is nowhere so full of dangerous things—
things that love dark places—
things that breathe only when you breathe
and hold their breath when I hold mine.
So I have to say:
"I'm not scared."
That face, grinning in the pattern on the wall
isn't a face—
"I'm not scared."
That prickle on the back of my neck
Is only the label on my pyjama jacket—
"I'm not scared."
That moaning moaning is nothing
but water in a pipe—
"I'm not scared."

Everything's going to be just fine
as soon as I get into that bed of mine.
Such a terrible shame
it's always the same
it takes so long
it takes so long
it takes so long
to get there.

From the light switch
to my bed.
It's the Longest Journey in the World.

*Michael Rosen*

# Go to Sleep

When I was a little boy and would not
go to bed when I was told, my parents
would warn me, "Go to sleep or the owl
will put you in his ear and fly away with you."
I asked them where the owl would take
me and what he would do with me.
They would not say.
So I would just lie there.
And try to figure it out for myself.
After thinking how the owl would go
about putting me in his ear and flying
away, I would fall asleep.
I still wonder where he would take me.

*Wayne Yerxa*

# Not Being Able to Sleep

The worst thing about
not being able to sleep
I think
is
when suddenly you realize
that you're not going to be able
to sleep.

*Siv Widerberg*

# Quite a Few Things

Quite a few things
haven't happened
to me yet,
I go to bed
too early.

*Richard J. Margolis*

# The Night

As I curl up to go to sleep
I have such lovely thoughts
The darkness of my room,
The warmness of my bed
And what the day has brought.

*Amy Goodman*

# Night Fun

I hear eating.
I hear drinking.
I hear music.
I hear laughter.
Fun is something
Grownups never have
Before my bedtime.
Only after.

*Judith Viorst*

# I Never Hear

I never hear my mother come
Into my room late, late at night.
She says she has to look and see
If I'm still tucked exactly right.
Nor do I feel her kissing me.
She says she does, though,
Every night.

*Dorothy Aldis*

# Very Very Quietly

Very very
quietly
I
got up
and stood
at the door
and listened.
They were talking about someone else.
I
went back
to bed.

*Richard J. Margolis*

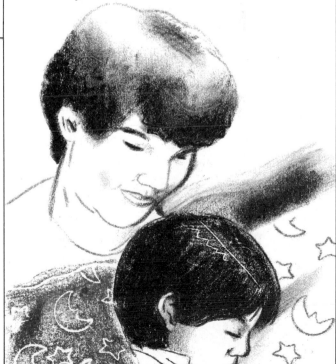

Bedtime. Not a pleasant thought for most of us, is it?

What stalling tactics do *you* use to put off that dreaded time? Here are some simple, successful ideas collected from his classmates by ten-year-old B.J. Montabello of Burnaby, British Columbia:

- Set all the clocks back two hours.
- Say your Science project this week is to measure how little sleep the human body requires, or that your Socials homework is to watch the 10 o'clock News.
- Create a skyscraper super-sub sandwich, and remind your parents that the school nurse says every mouthful of food has to be chewed thirty-two times.
- Brush your teeth until they glow in the dark.
- Play Haunted House tapes under your bed, then tell your parents your bedroom is haunted.

**1. By Yourself**

- Reread the poems in this Collection.
- Which one most closely describes the way you feel at bedtime?

**2. In a Small Group**

- Discuss your bedtimes with each other. Do you feel you go to bed too early? too late? at the right time?
- Do you think it's true that:
  "Early to bed, early to rise will make you healthy, wealthy, and wise"?
- Start your own collection of bedtime sayings. Ask your parents, grandparents, and neighbours if they can tell you any. Try to collect some from other countries.

**3. By Yourself**

Reread "Last One Into Bed." The author doesn't exaggerate: he doesn't tell us about imagining a ten-headed dragon with blood dripping from his teeth. Instead, he tells us what he has really imagined. It isn't a real thing, but it is a real imagining: "That face, grinning in the pattern on the wall."

And that's how he gets us to feel what he's feeling. We have all imagined faces in patterns: we can understand that.

- Make a list of real things that your imagination could make scary, e.g., the wind moving your blinds, or creaky bedsprings. What could these things be?
- Put this list on one half of a large sheet of paper. List what these real things *could* be on the other side.
- Practise reading the real things in a normal voice and practise reading the scary things in a spooky voice.
- Make your list into a poem. Say your poem to a partner.

**4. In a Small Group**
- Reread "Not Being Able to Sleep."
- What is the worst thing about bedtime for you? What is the best? Why?
- What special tricks do you have for putting yourself to sleep? Dramatize your special tricks for another group.

**5. With the Whole Class**
- Read "Night Fun" again. Do you agree with the poet? Give your reasons.
- What do the grown-ups in your home do after you've gone to bed? Imagine a change in the bedtime routine: the adults go to bed early and the kids stay up late.
- What would you do? Write down your ideas. Shape the list into a poem.
- Reread "Go to Sleep." Do you use stalling tactics to delay your bedtime? What do you say or do? How do the adults respond? Make a list of these stalling tactics, and use this list to write a poem entitled "How I Avoid Going to Bed."

**6. By Yourself**
- Write a bedtime poem of your own. It could be about how you feel when you're falling asleep, how you avoid going to bed, any scary things you think of at bedtime, or it could even be a lullabye.

# BROTHERS AND SISTERS

**With the Whole Class**
- How many in the class are the youngest children in their families? How many are the oldest? How many are in the middle? How many are only children?
- Discuss the advantages and disadvantages of having brothers and sisters; of being a younger sibling, an older sibling, an only child.

**In a Small Group**
- Invent your own brother or sister! Make this person the best brother or sister you can possibly imagine. (Will this person be older or younger than you?)
- Write down words that describe how the person looks. Draw the person. Give him or her a name.
- On your drawing, write down words and phrases that describe what's so special about this brother or sister.

# I'm the Youngest in Our House

I'm the youngest in our house
so it goes like this:

My brother comes in and says:
"Tell him to clear the fluff
out from under his bed."
Mum says,
"Clear the fluff
out from under your bed."
Father says,
"You heard what your mother said."
"What?" I say.
"The fluff," he says.
"Clear the fluff
out from under your bed."
So I say,
"There's fluff under his bed, too,
you know."

So father says,
"But we're talking about the fluff
under your bed."
"You will clear it up
won't you?" mum says.
So now my brother—all puffed up—
says,
"Clear the fluff
out from under your bed,
clear the fluff
out from under your bed."
Now I'm angry. I am angry.
so I say—what shall I say?
I say,
"Shuttup stinks

YOU CAN'T RULE MY LIFE."

*Michael Rosen*

# Moochie

Moochie likes to keep on playing
That same old silly game
Peeka Boo!
Peeka Boo!

I get tired of it
But it makes her laugh
And every time she laughs
She gets the hiccups
And every time she gets the hiccups
I laugh

*Eloise Greenfield*

# Little Sister

Little sister
holds on tight.
My hands hurt
from all that squeezing,
but I don't mind.
She thinks no one will bother her
when I'm around,
and they won't
if I can help it.
And even when I can't,
I try
'cause she believes in me.

*Nikki Grimes*

# My Brother and I

If we were good friends
we would talk to each other,
but since we're related,
you're only my brother.

We share the same roof,
the same clothes, the same bike
and to think we rode
on the very same trike.

We see each other every day
and love each other in a small private way.

If we were good friends,
we would talk to each other,
but since we're related,
you're only my brother.

*Joan Turchan*

# Smarties

Smarties . . . M-m-m . . .
    Mine go first (as usual)
    while my big sister Alice
    just gets started hers.

"My box wasn't full," I complain. I'm sure.
    That Smartie Company
    isn't so smart after all.

"That can't happen **every** time," argues Alice,
    smacking her lips
    on the Smarties that come endlessly—
    neverendingly—
    from her box.
"You just eat yours too fast."

She sucks each Smartie,
    and slurps,
    and licks;
examines the purple ones.
    Sorts out the yellows
    and puts them in a delicious little pile
    that sits there longingly,
    wishing they were mine.
She makes another pile:
    "I don't like the brown ones"—
    her voice is flat and bored.

I try not to be too eager,
    too ready,
    too wanting.
"I'll eat them, I don't mind."

She doesn't even blink:
"No, you won't. You gulped yours,
    greedy pig."

"But I'll help you with the brown."

"NO YOU WON'T!"

"Sure, c'mon, just one or two."

She wets a red one with her spit
    and leans low into the gleaming chrome
    of the toaster,
    catching the reflection of her fat lips
    as she smears the red
    like lipstick.

"Mom won't like that red on you!" I bleat,
    wishing I could eat the reds,
    or mauves,
    or even the browns.

Alice snorts,
    eyes me: the irritating fly
    that she might use the fly swat on .
    swift and quick;
    or the Raid . . .
    and slowly watch me squirm.

"**If** you beg," says Alice.
    "Down on all fours—
    no, on your belly on the floor
    like Rover does for doggie treats."

"NO WAY!" I scream.
    "You can't make me—I'll tell Mom—
    It's not fair! You **never** share with me!"

"You want the browns?" tempts the
    unrelenting Alice.
    "So BEG down on your belly."

I drop to my knees,
    feel the doggie hair growing on my paws.
    My ears grow long and fluffy.
    My tongue lolls out.

"Roll over," commands Alice.
    I roll.

"Sit — no, sing."
    "Aw, c'mon, Alice . . ."

"SING."
    I howl, and yowl, and whine
    a Rover song.
    Then Alice carelessly tosses
    a brown Smartie.

I scramble, snatch it up —
    "NO HANDS!" screams Alice.
    "Just with your tongue
    or else — no more . . .
    and I've got a pink one here for you."

I lick the brown one off the floor.
    And whine for more
    Smarties.

*Deborah Staudinger*

Families! Like it or not, we all have them. They're there when we really need them, and they're there when we don't. They're the people who know us the best. They know how to comfort us when we're feeling down. They know the special things that will make us feel better. They also know what will really make us mad—and sometimes they do just that to tease us.

*1. In a Small Group*
- Read the poems in this Collection again.
- Now, read them aloud to each other.
- Experiment with ways to make the readings more lively and interesting to listen to.

*2. With a Partner*
- Imagine you are the two people in "Smarties." How would *you* get your older sister to give you some of her smarties: think about what you would say, what she would say back to you; what you would do, what she would do.
- Use your ideas to make up a dialogue or a little play.
- Perform it for another set of partners.

*3. In a Small Group*
- Reread "My Brother and I."
- The poet doesn't talk to his brother as he does to his friends. Why do you think this might be?
- Do you think differently about family members than you do about friends? Do you have different feelings? Do you behave differently, too? What are some of these differences? Why do they exist?

**4. With a Partner**

- Reread "I'm the Youngest in Our House."
- Do you think what happens in the poem is fair? Why or why not?
- How do you think each person in the poem should behave?
- Write your own ending for the poem. Begin after the line "There's fluff under his bed, too, you know."
- Or, write your own poem, beginning:

  I'm the _____ in our house
  so it goes like this:

- Practise reading your poem. Decide who will read what. Use lots of expression.
- Read your poem to another set of partners. How do your endings compare?

**5. In a Small Group**

- Read "Little Sister" again. How does the poet feel about her little sister? How does the little sister feel?
- Do you have feelings like that for people you know? Do people have these feelings for you?
- What other strong feelings do you have for people in your family? Focus on your feelings for one member of your family. Jot down some of these feelings. Shape them into a poem. You might begin:

  You are my _____
  And this is how I feel about you:

**6. By Yourself**

- Think about the way in which the sisters in "Little Sister" hold hands and the feelings that expresses.
- What do *you* do that lets someone in your family know how *you* feel about him or her?
- Write a poem about this: focus on one incident.
- Share your poem with a partner. Can your partner tell what feeling you're expressing?

# friend dog

# *GETTING READY!*

*By Yourself*
- Since you were a young child, you've had plenty of real or imaginary friends — people, pets, stuffed animals, someone in a song, book, or dream.
- Put down the names of some of your friends, past or present.
- Beside each name, write down a few things that remind you of your friend . . .
  a description; something you did together; some place you went together.
- Look over what you have written. Choose one friend.
- Using the ideas you wrote down, write a poem to this friend. This is a ''dedication.''
- Practise reading the poem aloud.

*With the Whole Class*
- Listen to each other's dedications!
  *P.S.* Don't forget to applaud everyone's special friend.

*from* **"friend dog"**

dog

    you
    are my friend
and
    i
    am your
        friend
dog

we are for
each
    other

last spring

      you found me    in the back field
      and i
        found you
the wild dogs
had
   used your ear    to chew a message

          stay
        away

we took you to the vet

for shots and healing creams
        and put you
        in  a  box
beside the washing machine
    where it was
      warm

you dreamed your fighting
      chasing
        dreams

big sister and mama
            and    papa
and me    worked hard on afternoons
        to
            build your run    with a wire fence
                            around    it

            your house with shingles
                        on the roof

inside your house

                dishes and bowls
                                and
                rawhide chewing
                            bones
an old
        toy turtle    that beeped
                        when you bit
                            his head

a pillow for your bed

friend    and    dog

                            because
you are both

and they
        are both the same
that
    is
    your
    name

    dog
                you
                are so black
        your
                coat
                your
                coat
                is black

        inside the hair
                you
                are
                    blue

        dog

            you
            are so smart
    sometimes
                    you
                    are
        girl
                    and
    sometimes

    i can be dog

105

when we are sitting on that flat
                    rock

and you look at me      and i look
                         at you
          i know we are talking
                    to each other

                    i just speak
                    for  us  both

my job

          to bring fresh water and food
          new
          straw
          for the inside
          of your house
your job
          to eat and drink
                    and grow    strong
          to
          sleep safe and warm
          through the cold
                    night

                    dream right

friend dog

          even in this winter time
your morning
               bark will bring me
                              out
                         of bed
for my breakfast
                    and
your
walk

106

jumping

  into bowls
is your
  best thing
and warm
  wet licks
    on
    my
cold
face

mama says

  if i travel far and put you down
  you
  can
    go a thousand miles
      to find me
and
our
 place

we can take you
  out

    around the yard
where you can
  see your run
    and your
     house
  and we can practice
    staying
     close
when i take off the leash

the run

the house the bowls of food and water
the
  fresh straw my hugs and your hurt
      ear
      are telling
      you
there is no
better
  place    stay near

*Arnold Adoff*

Do you have a dog? Or have you ever had one? If not, chances are you've at least wanted one. Dogs are probably the oldest and best-loved pets.

But over the years, and among different peoples, dogs have been more than just pets. Ancient peoples in many places worshipped their dogs. People in the Australian outback wore their dogs as cover against the cold: a chilly night was known as a "three-dog night." In more recent times, dogs have been kept as hunters, as herders of sheep and cattle, as guards, as guides, as sled dogs. They've also been kept to perform tricks and stunts, to act, or just to show.

For most of us though, it is as pet and companion that we best know and love friend dog.

1. *With a Partner*
   - Reread "Friend Dog" silently.
   - Now, read the poem aloud to each other. Take turns reading.
   - In your own words, retell the story to each other: one tells it from the viewpoint of the dog's owner; the other tells it from the viewpoint of the dog.

2. *By Yourself or With a Partner*
   - Discuss and write down each other's ideas about these questions:
     Why do people have pets?
     What pets do they keep?
     What makes a good pet owner?
     What makes a good pet?
     What makes a pet become a friend?
   - Dramatize your answers in the form of a pet store owner selling a pet to someone. Make it silly? sad? serious? funny?

3.   *With a Partner*   • Think of an animal, real or imagined, that you'd both really like to have.
• Make up a "Pet Wanted" poster for this animal. Draw a picture of the pet. Describe how it should look and how it should behave. (Your poster can be funny or serious.)
• Display your poster.
• Take a class vote to choose the most-wanted pet.

4.a) *With a Partner*   • Think of an animal or a person who means as much to you as Friend Dog means to the poet.
• Talk about your friend: describe him or her; tell about how you met; tell of some of the special things you and your friend do for each other; recall a good time you shared with your friend; describe something you and your friend really like to do together.
• While you talk about your friend, your partner should write down some of the important words you use.

b) *By Yourself*   • Look at the words that your partner wrote down. Make up sentences using some of these words. Play with them till they sound right to you. Put them in an order that tells a story. Try to shape them into a short poem.
• Read over your poem to see if it says what you really wanted it to say about you and your friend.

c) *With a Partner*   • Ask your partner (not the one you first talked to about your friend) to read your poem.
• Have your partner tell you what he or she knows about you and your friend after reading your poem.
• Has your friend got the message you wanted to give? Why or why not? If your partner doesn't understand what you really wanted to say, you may want to change your poem.

# PLEASE...
# AND
# THANK YOU

***In a Small Group***

- Think of times when someone has told you, "Don't do that! It's bad manners!" Did you understand why? Did you agree?
- Can something be bad manners in one situation but not in another?
- Do you think manners are important?

***With a Partner***

- What does it mean to have good manners? How do people learn good manners? From whom?
- Make a list of all the things you *could* do that would show bad manners.
- Make this list the basis for a little comic book that teaches someone *good* manners.
- Display your comic book so others can read it.

## Company Manners

Hands off the tablecloth
Don't rumble belly
Don't grab for grub
Don't slurp the soup
Don't crumble the crackers
Don't mash the mushrooms
Don't mush the potatoes
Don't stab the steak
Don't slap the saltshaker
Don't pill the bread
Don't swill the sauce
Don't ooze the mayonnaise
Don't slop the slaw
Don't spatter the ketchup
Don't gulp the olives
Don't spit the pits
Don't finger the lettuce
Don't dribble dressing
Don't chomp the celery
Don't gobble the cobbler
Don't guzzle the fizz
Swallow, don't swig
Don't smack your lips
Pat with a napkin
Daintily dab
Quietly quaff
Fastidiously sip
And gracefully sample
a nibbling tidbit.

*Eve Merriam*

## Learning

I'm learning to say thank you.
And I'm learning to say please.
And I'm learning to use Kleenex,
Not my sweater when I sneeze.
And I'm learning not to dribble.
And I'm learning not to slurp.
And I'm learning (though it
sometimes really hurts me)
Not to burp.
And I'm learning to chew softer
When I eat corn on the cob.
And I'm learning that it's much
Much easier to be a slob.

*Judith Viorst*

# First Banquet

Grandad retired,
and all the
employees held
a banquet
in his honour.

Even I was
invited.
I wore my
best red dress,
and Mom
put my hair
back in
French braids.

The table
was beautiful,
alight with
tall white
candles
on a long
white
table cloth.
I sat
next to Grandma.
People chatted,
wine glasses clinked,
forks stabbed
pieces of chicken.

And then,
without warning,
it happened.

My hand
reached over,
picked up
what it thought
to be a
fancy dessert,
and moved
toward
my mouth.

In one
irreversible moment
I bit off
the head
of a paper napkin,
a paper napkin
someone had
cleverly twisted
into the
shape of a
swan.

*Pal Thompson*

# Etiquette

Is having respect
when you
eat everything
your grandmother
has put on the plate
even the eggs
that run white
and gluey
like the stuff
out of squished
caterpillars?

*Carolyn Mamchur*

# It Takes All Kinds

We know some kids
Who said, "No thank you,"
When Dad asked them
To have some candy.
Very nice kids, too.
Some things are hard
To figure out.
Weren't they hungry?
Didn't they like candy?
Or what?

*Mary Neville*

## How to Dive for Pearls and Avoid Eating Your Peas

Remember that peas are pearls
and you are a pearl diver.

Mashed potatoes are coral
and form a tropical lagoon.

The gravy is the ocean
that fills the lagoon.

Drop the pearls into the lagoon.

Dive for pearls.
Surface.

Let the ocean trickle from your chin,
and wait to bc dismissed
from the table.

*Patrick Keeney*

## Old Joke

'Look at your hands!'
The teacher cried.
'Couldn't be dirtier
If you tried.
What would you say
If mine were like this?'
'We'd be too polite
To mention it, Miss!''

*Allan Ahlberg*

Manners. What are they exactly? Here is one example: What do you think of it?

"It's important to be just as courteous when leaving the room (or being asked to leave a room) as you were when you entered," writes Bob Stine, author of *Don't Stand In the Soup: The World's Funniest Guide to Manners*. "Be sure to say goodbye with a broad smile and a hearty handshake. As you leave, try not to take items that everyone can plainly see do not belong to you.

"Here are three very polite phrases you may wish to memorize. They are sure to be useful at one time or another when saying goodbye.

1. 'No hard feelings. I'll be glad to pay for the damages.'
2. 'Bye now. I hope the swelling goes down real soon.'
3. 'Okay. All right. I can take a hint. I'm leaving.' "

**1. In a Small Group**

- Reread the poems silently to yourself. Then read them aloud to each other.
- Take a vote to find out which poem is the most favourite and which the least.
- Together, list the poems in order from most favourite to least favourite.
- Discuss what you liked most about your favourite poem, and what you didn't like about your least favourite.

**2. With a Partner**

- Talk about the poems. What does each poem have to say about manners?
- Find out what "etiquette" means. What's the difference between etiquette and good manners?
- Reread "Etiquette." Think of a time when you've had to say or do something you didn't want to. What happened? Did you display good manners? Write about it in a poem.

**3. By Yourself**

- Reread "How to Dive for Pearls and Avoid Eating Your Peas." In this poem, the poet imagines that peas are pearls.
- Choose a food that you don't like to eat and imagine that it's something pleasant. Write your own "How to _____ and Avoid Eating _____" poem. Begin with "Remember that is/are _____."

**4. With a Partner**

- Make up a "Checklist of Manners." Write down things to do and things not to do.
- Shape it into a poem for a younger person.

**5. By Yourself**

- Reread "First Banquet."
- Look at how the poet wrote it. It's like a little story filled with so many details it makes you feel you were right there.
- Write your own poem, just the way Pal Thompson wrote "First Banquet."
- Write about a real moment of embarrassment.

*P.S.* This can be a private poem for your private collection.

# ...BIG FAT WHOPPERS!

**With a Partner**
- Go through a newspaper or magazine and cut out a few short, interesting articles, cartoons, and advertisements.
- Rewrite certain parts of your collection . . . exaggerate some of the details . . . just enough to make each one into a big, fat whopper!
- Arrange your collection so that it looks like a page of a newspaper.

**With the Whole Class**
- Put everyone's pages together into a classroom newspaper called "The Big Fat Whopper."

**In a Small Group**
- Think about some little thing that happened while you were having breakfast this morning. Did you spill the milk? Step on the cat? Or think of something that happened on the way to school. (If you can't recall anything, make something up.)
- Exaggerate the incident to turn it into a big fat whopper.
- Make your big fat whopper into a verse.
- Write all the class's verses on a long sheet of paper and call it "Tall Tales."

## Lies

When we are bored
My friend and I
Tell
Lies.

It's a competition: the prize
Is won by the one
Whose lies
Are the bigger size.

We really do:
That's true.
But there isn't a prize:
That's lies.

*Kit Wright*

## The Pocket

i reached
into my
pocket
and much
to my
surprise
something in
there
grabbed me
and pulled
me right
inside
i felt
its clammy fingers
all bony
cold and
thin
i tried to
keep my
head out
no use
it all
went in
and that
was not

the end
of it
the pocket
seemed
so deep
and dark
and strange
and scary
i felt i
had to
weep
"shut up
you silly
creature"
a voice
yelled
in my
ear
and then
my feet
were
pulled inside
and i
had disappeared

*Sean O'Huigin*

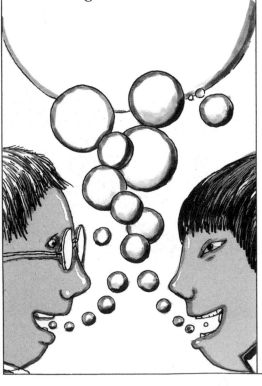

# Flight of the Roller-Coaster

Once more around should do it, the man confided . . .

And sure enough, when the roller-coaster reached the peak
Of the giant curve above me—screech of its wheels
Almost drowned by the shriller cries of the riders—

Instead of the dip and plunge with its landslide of screams
It rose in the air like a movieland magic carpet, some
                wonderful bird,

And without fuss or fanfare swooped slowly across the
                amusement park,
Over Spook's Castle, ice-cream booths, shooting-gallery;
          and losing no height

Made the last yards above the beach, where the cucumber-cool
Brakeman in the last seat saluted
A lady about to change from her bathing-suit

Then, as many witnesses duly reported, headed leisurely
              over the water,
Disappearing mysteriously all too soon behind a low-lying
            flight of clouds.

*Raymond Souster*

# When the Teacher Rang the Bell for Recess

I was so fastoutthedoor
I ate three doughnut holes and a tuna sandwich
Had two goes on the tyre swing
Zoomed across the playground on the trolley
And did a round of the bases
Before the teacher's hand
Finished ringing the bell for recess.

*Deborah Staudinger*

# *Now* I'll Have No Trouble

Grandpa and I
loved riding together:
the trouble was
he could never tell
our horses apart.

So Grandpa docked
his horse's tail.

Now *his* horse
had a short tail,
mine had a long tail,
and Grandpa could tell
our horses apart . . .
Until my horse
lost part of its tail
on a barbed wire fence.

So then Grandpa
nobbed his horse's ear.

Now, *his* horse
had a nobbed ear,
mine didn't,
and Grandpa could tell
our horses apart again . . .
until my horse
nicked its ear
on a tree branch.

So now Grandpa
*measured* the horses:
"Aha!" he cried out,
"*now* I'll have no trouble
telling them apart.
Looks like my white horse
is a head taller
than your black one."

*Meguido Zola*

# I Gotta Tell You

Hey, listen,
*listen*
**LISTEN!**
I gotta tell ya
'bout this weird thing
happen' a mee sayerday night—
like it's weird
it's *really* weird!
I just **gotta** tell ya—
Eh? Wassat?
You don' wanna know?
Oh . . . okay, okay.

*Zoë Guimaldo*

# Th Guy Drivin Round In

th vankouvr city pound
truck is giving me
sum strange
looks
so i
barkd at
him

*bill bissett*

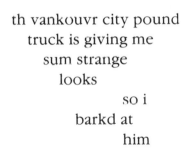

Whoppers? Whoppers?! What's a whopper? An oversize bunny? An uncontrollable desire for a hamburger? Or what?

To tell the truth, the poems in this unit are a pack of lies. Not ordinary lies, of course. That would never do.

No, these are poems that have just enough something in them to cause you to wonder if . . . well, if they *might* not be true after all. But, at the same time, they are poems that are so strange that you know that they just *couldn't* really have happened. They are poems that are the work of poets who lie just for the fun of it, and, now and then, for a serious purpose too.

**1. In a Small Group**
- Reread the poems in this Collection.
- Each person: chooses his or her favourite ''whoppers'' poem; practises reading it aloud; thinks of how to present the poem using mime or props.
- Take turns presenting your poems to the group.
- Let each reader know how you enjoyed the performance. What feedback can you offer that could improve the performance?

**2. In a Small Group**
- Each of the poems in this Collection is a lie of some kind.
- Read over ''Lies.'' What is a lie? What is the difference between a lie and a whopper or tall tale? Together, list as many different kinds of lies as you can think of—white lies, social lies, April fool jokes, hoaxes, tall tales, exaggerations—and why people tell them. Look again at the other poems in this unit to help you. Use a dictionary, and any other references.
- What makes each of the poems in this Collection a whopper of some kind? What is true or real in each poem? What is fantasy? How do you know?
- Do you think it is wrong to tell lies? To tell whoppers? Sometimes? Always? Never? Give reasons for your answers.

- Make a book of all your lies and call it "A Pack of Lies! The Real Truth." Can you make it look like a "pack"?
- Or list reasons For Telling Whoppers and Reasons For Not Telling Lies. Shape the lists into two poems. Read them to another group.

*3. By Yourself*

- Reread "Flight of the Roller-Coaster." The poet imagines that when the roller-coaster reaches the top of the track, it takes off like a magic carpet. Children often pretend, or *fantasize*, that one object is another. A chair, for example, becomes a rocket.
- Try to remember a fantasy like this that you had as a small child. What was the real object and what did it become? Use this as the basis for a poem. To help you write your poem, you might think about questions such as: How did it move? Where did it go? What could you see? What happened?
- Reread "*Now* I'll Have No Trouble." Write a whopper about a larger-than-life person, a tall-tale hero or heroine. Your poem might focus on one or more of your hero's or heroine's appearance, dress, speech, actions, deeds, etc. Tell about some of the unbelievable feats he or she can do or has done. How were these things done? Why? With what consequences?

# Acknowledgements

Every effort has been made to trace the ownership of all copyright material and to secure the necessary permissions to reprint these selections. In the event of any question arising as to the use of any material, the editor and publisher, while expressing regret for any inadvertent error, will be happy to make the necessary correction in future printings.

The editor and publisher make grateful acknowledgement for permission to reprint the following copyrighted material. Material used in this anthology is grouped by author and listed in the order in which its author first appears.

"Chocolate," "Eats," "Not Me But," and "My Mouth" from EATS by Arnold Adoff. Copyright © 1979 by Arnold Adoff. By permission of Lothrop, Lee & Shepard Books (A Division of William Morrow & Company). "Friend Dog" excerpted from the book FRIEND DOG by Arnold Adoff. Text copyright © 1980 by Arnold Adoff (J.B. Lippincott Co.). By permission of Harper & Row Publishers, Inc.

"Poem for Aelurophobe," "What the 500 Kilogram Canary Said," "What's Red and Goes Ding Dong?" and "When They Give Me . . ." by Marah Gilead. Copyright © 1988 by Marah Gilead and Copp Clark Pitman (A Longman Company).

"Place Names" by Meguido Zola from HIYOU TUMTUM. Copyright © 1978 by Meguido Zola. "Apple For Teacher," "Knock-Knock. Who's There?" and "Now I'll Have No Trouble" by Meguido Zola. Copyright © 1988 by Meguido Zola and Copp Clark Pitman (A Longman Company). "One Hamburger Please" by Meguido Zola, first published in IMPRESSIONS (Holt, Rinehart and Winston of Canada), 1984, by permission of the author.

"Gift Wrapped" by Inge Israel. Copyright © by Inge Israel.

"5-4-3" and "My Dad's Thumb" from MIND YOUR BUSINESS by Michael Rosen. "Chocolate Cake" from QUICK LET'S GET OUT OF HERE by Michael Rosen. "Last One Into Bed" from YOU CAN'T CATCH ME by Michael Rosen. "I'm The Youngest In Our House" from WOULDN'T YOU LIKE TO KNOW by Michael Rosen. Copyright © by Michael Rosen, 1974, 1977, 1981, and 1983. Reprinted by permission of the author and Andre Deutsch Ltd. "The Hardest Thing To Do In The World" by Michael Rosen from YOU TELL ME by Roger McGough and Michael Rosen (Kestrel Books, 1979), Michael Rosen poems: copyright © by Michael Rosen. Collection copyright © 1979 by Penguin Books Ltd. Reproduced by permission of Penguin Books Ltd.

"Lost" by Shaunt Basmajian from HERE IS A POEM edited by Florence McNeil. Copyright © 1983, by Shaunt Basmajian. By permission of the author and The League of Canadian Poets.

"Dad and The Cat and The Tree" and "Lies," from RABBITING ON by Kit Wright. Copyright © 1978 by Kit Wright. By permission of William Collins Sons & Co. Ltd.

"Canada Day" from TICK BIRD by George Swede. Copyright © 1974 by George Swede. By permission of the author and Three Trees Press.

"Nature" by Milton Acorn. Copyright © by Milton Acorn. By permission of the author.

"Who Was Left?" collected by Brandy Longstaffe; "Batty Books" collected by Ralph Smith; "What Does?" collected by Katie Krajina; "What's In Your Lunchkit?" collected by Gail Fisher; "Becky Babcock" collected by Becky Babcock; "Which Is The Witch?" collected by Gail Fisher; "Mia Mama" collected by George Vallesquez; "A Tall Girl" collected by Cami Watts; "The Skunk" collected by Miki Zibarras; "Peter Piper" collected by Wolfgang Hufnagel; "Un Chasseur" collected by Chloé Raunet; "Betty Batter" collected by Amanda Chalmers; "How Many Cans?" collected by Joe Luterbach; "Friendship Rhyme" collected by Ulara Nakagawa; "Taunts and Teases" collected by Ajit Singh; "Chants and Cheers" collected by Anabel Alvarez; "Skipping Rhymes" collected by Cherie Plante; "Counting Out Rhymes" collected by Sean McLeod; "Holes" collected by Joe Rigadelle. "Out In The Field" collected by Cami Watts; "It's Yours" collected by Pippa Emrick; "It's In" collected by Antoinette Keenleyside; "Thirty White Horses" collected by Claudio Francescan; "It Has" collected by Cherie Plante; "A Room" collected by Melanie Boucher; and "Two Legs" collected by Maryka Pretzen. Copyright © by Copp Clark Pitman (A Longman Company).

"Doctor, Doctor" and "I Gotta Tell Ya" by Zoë Guimaldo. Copyright © 1986 and 1988 by Zoë Guimaldo and Copp Clark Pitman (A Longman Company).

"Yellow Butter" from YELLOW BUTTER PURPLE JELLY RED JAM BLACK BREAD by Mary Ann Hoberman. Copyright © 1981 by Mary Ann Hoberman. Reprinted by permission of Viking Penguin Inc.

"Sink Song" by J.A. Lindon. By permission of the author's estate.

"The Fastest Train In The World" by Keith Bosley from AND I DANCE. Reprinted with the permission of Angus & Robertson (UK) Ltd.

"TurningWheelsTurning," "Cartwheels," "Jigsaw Puddle," and "Courage" by Emily Hearn. Copyright © by Emily Hearn. By permission of the author.

"Toaster Time" from THERE IS NO RHYME FOR SILVER by Eve Merriam. Copyright © 1962 by Eve Merriam. "Sometimes" from JAMBOREE: RHYMES FOR ALL TIMES by Eve Merriam. Copyright © 1962, 1964, 1966, 1973, 1984 by Eve Merriam and "Company Manners" from OUT LOUD (Atheneum) by Eve Merriam. Copyright © 1973 by Eve Merriam. By permission of the author and Marian Reiner, for the author.

"The Washing Machine" by Jeffrey Davis. Copyright © by Jeffrey Davis. By permission of the author.

"Black Dot" by Libby Houston. Copyright © by Libby Houston. By permission of the author.

"Look" by John Smith, from A DISCREET IMMORALITY. Copyright © by John Smith. Reprinted by permission of Granada Publishing Limited.

"Summer" from COUNTRY PIE by Frank Asch. Copyright © 1979 by Frank Asch. By permission of Greenwillow Books (A Division of William Morrow & Company.)

## Index of Poems

## Answers to riddles

*Page 39:* An egg
Five hundred pairs of pants
Smoke

*Page 40:* **Holes** — because he was tired of the "hole" business
— a hole
**Out in the Field** — a watermelon

*Page 41:* **It's Yours** — your name
**It's In** — the letter "r"
**Thirty White Horses** — teeth
**It Has** — a cow

*Page 42:* **A Room** — a mushroom
**Two Legs** — a person sits on a three-legged stool, holding a chicken leg. A dog/cat runs in, grabs the chicken leg and runs. The person throws the stool at the dog/cat and makes it bring back the chicken leg.

1 2 3 4 5   4703-4   92 91 90 89